PROMISED LANDS

PAUL VALLELY was commended as International Reporter of the Year for his reports on the Ethiopian famine of 1984-85 for *The Times*. He accompanied Bob Geldof on a trip across Africa to decide how the proceeds of Live Aid should be spent, and wrote *With Geldof in Africa* as a result. Afterwards he co-wrote Geldof's autobiography, *Is That It?*, and has since written *Bad Samaritans: First World Ethics and Third World Debt*. He is a trustee of Traidcraft plc, which markets Third World goods in the UK and pays fair prices to their producers.

MIKE GOLDWATER is a founder member of the British photo-journalism agency Network Photographers. He undertakes assignments in Europe, Africa, Asia and South and Central America, for major magazines in the UK and abroad. His book *Fighting the Famine* is a photographic exploration of the causes and effects of famine in the Sahel. In 1989 a trip to Pakistan with Imran Khan produced the book *Indus Journey*. In 1991 Mike Goldwater won the Tom Hopkinson Photojournalist of the Year award.

D0315979

Promised Lands

Stories of Power and Poverty in the Third World

PAUL VALLELY

photographs by
MIKE GOLDWATER

WITH A FOREWORD BY JONATHON PORRITT

 Fount
An Imprint of HarperCollinsPublishers  **Christian Aid**

For Heather

PHOTOGRAPHS

Cover: A farmer ploughs his fields in the highlands of Eritrea, to the north of Ethiopia, while his sons dig drainage ditches in the hope that this year enough rain will fall to allow him to stay on his homeland.

Half title: A young sugar cane cutter, his face covered against the burning midday sun, on the Hacienda Luisita estate owned by the family of President Cory Aquino in the Philippines

Title page: A middle-aged woman on the wide dry plain of Meshal in the highlands of Eritrea where, according to ancient custom, village land is redivided and redistributed every seven years. But after a decade of drought the old ways are under threat.

Page 6: A *favela* child outside her makeshift home in São Paulo, Brazil.

Page 8: The pattern of the rice paddies of the Igorot tribal peoples in the Philippines are thousands of years old. But age-old systems of land-holding are being undermined by Western notions of ownership introduced during the colonial period and still spreading today to more remote areas like this one in the Mountain Province. In the background the fields are dotted with grain stores.

First published in Great Britain in 1992 by
Fount Paperbacks and Christian Aid

Fount Paperbacks is an imprint of
HarperCollins*Religious*
Part of HarperCollins*Publishers*
77–85 Fulham Palace Road, London W6 8JB

Copyright © 1992 Christian Aid

Paul Vallely and Mike Goldwater assert the moral right to be identified as the author and photographer of this work

Printed and bound in Great Britain by
HarperCollinsManufacturing Glasgow

A catalogue record for this book is available from the British Library

ISBN 0 00 627608 3

Conditions of Sale
This book is sold subject to the condition
that it shall not, by way of trade or otherwise,
be lent, re-sold, hired out or otherwise circulated
without the publisher's prior consent in any form of
binding or cover other than that in which it is
published and without a similar condition
including this condition being imposed
on the subsequent purchaser.

How much more time will you waste before
taking possession of the land which
the God of your fathers has given you?

JOSHUA 18:3

Promised Lands was commissioned in memory of
JANET LACEY,
Christian Aid's first director and
a tireless crusader for a world with a fair share for all.

Contents

Foreword

BY JONATHON PORRITT

'Go to the roots. Put your faith in local people. Speak the truth.'

It's so easy to be overwhelmed by despair when contemplating the sheer scale of human suffering amongst the world's poor. The statistics are so dehumanizing, the lack of resources so dispiriting. For all the best endeavours of all the development organizations, there is a widespread feeling that progress in alleviating such poverty has been negligible.

But despair is a self-indulgence, for it engenders resignation and passivity. Better by far that the fate of the world's poor should fill us again and again with anger instead.

And *Promised Lands* did indeed make me angry. Not just at the injustice and inhumanity that afflict the individuals it portrays, but at our own continuing collective acceptance of such injustice and inhumanity.

And I don't just mean that we go on allowing successive governments to posture as humanitarians, when both the level and the use of official aid budgets (*our* money, as Ministers keep on reminding us) remain wholly unsatisfactory. The latest figures from the Overseas Development Administration indicate that the UK's aid budget has now sunk below 0.3 per cent of GNP – way short of the United Nations' target figure of 0.7 per cent, and even further from what is now actually required.

But what also worries me is that even those who *do* care and who *are* angry are not necessarily responding in appropriate ways. Hence my delight in a book that upholds these values.

1   GO TO THE ROOTS

First, go to the roots of the problem, however daunting a process that may be, and however tempting it may be to keep on merely mitigating the symptoms.

At the root of much poverty today is landlessness. In country after country, historical patterns of inequitable land ownership have been maintained and even worsened in the post-war period. In poorer, largely agricultural, societies, to be without land is to be at the mercy of every local economic downturn and every vicissitude of the world economic order. To own land is to enjoy security, dignity and the potentiality for improving one's lot.

The author's account of the land distribution programme in Eritrea is as powerful a reminder as one might need of the knock-on benefits of people having access to land. Such programmes work as powerful multipliers of social and economic benefits throughout the community.

2   PUT YOUR FAITH IN LOCAL PEOPLE

Slowly, still too slowly, Western aid agencies are renouncing that old arrogance that made their presence in many Third World countries such a mixed blessing. I was deeply impressed to discover Christian Aid, in the three countries featured in this book, working for people by working with them, making use of rather than discounting local expertise, local knowledge and local commitment. 'Development at the grassroots' is a pretty nebulous concept, but it comes vibrantly alive through the voices of this book's protagonists.

3   SPEAK THE TRUTH

Easily said, but not easy to do. At a time when some people are intent on tying aid agencies down to 'begging bowl charity' (wait 'til the bowl is proffered, fill it, and ask not why the bowl is being used or why, inevitably, it will have to be used again some time soon), it's heartening to read such a rational yet uncompromising analysis of some of the causes of poverty and of the need to confront the political realities which cause such poverty.

The UK Government is said to be increasingly keen to tie future aid budgets to improved human rights and greater efforts to strengthen democracy. All well and good. But just as important a form of 'conditionality' would be to tie such budgets to programmes of progressive land reform.

Though preferable to despair, anger can and often does become negative. Even the anger of compassion. But not when tied to a resilient faith in human nature and to examples of voluntary donations being used in such practical and realistic ways. Then it helps us to work out our own priorities, and to strengthen our resolve to be *active* in whatever way is most appropriate. And this book does just that.

Jonathon Porritt
4 November 1991

1 | Life without Land

The struggle of the poor to grow their own food

It is an image for our civilization and our time. Outside the old man, his back bent, strains with a spade, as his father did before him, lifting potatoes from the sandy soil. Inside the house sits his son, the poet, listening to the clean rasp of the spade as it cuts through the living roots of the grass. The father digs, the son writes, comparing the spade to his pen. 'I've no spade to follow men like them,' concludes Seamus Heaney.

Like all great poets he speaks for many more people than himself. Today in the Western world most of us are estranged from the land which produces the food which sustains us. To us land is a garden, an allotment, a field in the countryside through which we drive. It is a place of relaxation or recreation or therapy.

This is not the case for most people in the world. Land to them is as vital to daily survival as it was to the poet's father and to the forefathers of most of us. Throughout the Third World – where two thirds of the earth's population lives – to have land can mean the difference between life and death. Those who have land, or who have access to it and have the tools to cultivate it, can use it to produce what they need to feed themselves and their family. It lessens their dependency on the availability of work or on the goodwill of others. It renders them less likely to perish because of an emergency or illness which most of us would regard as quite minor. It gives them something in which to invest labour, care, ingenuity and knowledge and perhaps even spare cash. The landless are that much more vulnerable.

Every day some 35,000 mothers watch their children die for lack of food in a world which produces enough food for all its inhabitants. Millions more see their children's growth stunted by malnutrition, for one in five of the world's total population eats inadequately for at least part of every year. Those without land figure with terrible prominence in these statistics of starvation.

It is easy for those of us in the industrialized world to forget the extent to which our survival depends upon what is produced by the land. We are shielded by the superstructure of a sophisticated economy. Our food comes from supermarkets, and an increasing amount of it is imported from the other side of the globe. We pay for it with wages earned in jobs mostly connected with selling services and goods to others. Those who are poor are usually supported by the safety net of a welfare state which, while it does not abolish indignity, nonetheless eradicates the horror of starvation – and even the poor are largely remote from the land. A long chain of human and social activity insulates almost everyone in our society from those who produce from the land on our behalf.

For most of the people in the world the experience is much more direct. And if their sense of contact with the land is much more immediate, so is their sense of dependency on it. In developing countries sixty per cent of the population work on the land – in the poorest countries that percentage is much higher, more than eighty per cent in most African countries.

Many work to provide us with the raw materials for our food and clothing but many more labour with the hope of producing enough simply to survive.

Every year more and more people on this planet are dependent for their daily needs on what they can produce from the land. In 1965 some 741 million people relied directly on the land for their daily bread; in 1982 the figure was about 1,250 million; in 1991 it was estimated to be around 2,496 million. Even those who do have a small plot often cannot make a living from it. Prices for their crops fall. The cost of seeds and other essentials may rise. They may have to resort to desperate short-term measures which yield something this year but destroy the land for future harvests. A year of poor rain, or an illness in the family, may mean they must sell their land and become landless too.

For a huge number of the world's population, therefore, land is more than just the place where they work or build their home. It is the generator of new life and as such is a symbol of hope. Their ability to take control of their own lives is, therefore, to a great extent determined by their access to land and their ability to farm it.

This is something which has been common to poor people throughout the ages. To the oppressed people of Israel enslaved in Egypt it was a Promised Land which was the great symbol of hope – and it is no coincidence that this is the biblical story which has most resonance for many of the poor throughout Asia, Africa and Latin America today. It is interesting, as one Brazilian theologian pointed out to me, that in the Old Testament the Hebrew word which is most used when speaking of the Promised Land is not *'erets*, which means land in the sense of territory, but *'adamah*, which has a much wider and richer meaning encompassing agricultural land which can sustain life. It is in this sense that land is life and to deny people access to it is

to withdraw from them the wherewithal to live.

But today there are more people on the planet without land, or without sufficient land to sustain themselves, than ever before. This book sets out to find out why and asks what can be done about it. But it is not a book about economic or social theory. It is a book about people, their stories and their struggles. So it is with people we will begin. And to understand the complexity of the phenomenon of landlessness we will first look at five individuals who confront the problem in very different situations.

Virgilina's Story

It was the same treatment for toothache which her great-grandmother had brought from Europe. There had been no advances in medical technology since the 19th century when her family had left their peasant life in Italy and set out with great hopes for a new life in Brazil where they had heard that there was good land in plenty for all. She tied a large piece of cloth under her chin and fastened it on top of her head.

'It keeps the jaw warm and it helps the pain a little. The tooth will either get better or it will fall out,' she smiled, with grim humour. It was her only smile of the morning and it revealed that she had had toothache many times before. Rotten brown gaps were almost as common as teeth in her mouth.

The effect of the cloth would have been comic had it not been for the sadness in her soft brown eyes. It affronted her sense of dignity to be seen by an outsider like this. She turned away and picked up her baby Heronisa.

The child's romper suit was terribly grubby but there were no other clothes to change her into. And it was winter, and too cold to leave the four-month-old lying in underclothes while she washed and dried the outfit. The same was true of the torn and patched clothes of the other five children. All had changed colour with the worn-in grime.

Virgilina and her husband Quintino live at the side of the road in the Mediterranean climate zone of Brazil in the southern state of Paraná. Their home is like a big garden shed in structure, except that its roof and walls are made only of black plastic sheets. The floor is of damp brown earth, the colour of dark chocolate. On it they have a table and dresser which were handed down to them from the days when Brazil looked as if it might fulfil its promise to the European immigrants. But the kitchen utensils revealed the downward slide of the generations; they were made of old cans and things others had thrown away.

'My father had a little bit of land but when there was sickness in the family he got into debt to pay doctors' bills and had to sell the land,' said Quintino. 'He became a day labourer, finding somewhere to live where he worked. At first I did that too but now there is less and less work. The big landowners are buying more and more of the land and turning it over from farming to cattle. I have had no work for a month despite the fact that I walk for miles every week around the farms asking for some casual work. The next we can expect is after the harvest: we are allowed to go along after the mechanical harvester, gleaning by hand, on condition that we give half of what we glean to the landowner.'

A pretty little blonde girl ran up and asked her mother for something to eat. Dionise was six. She had soft light hair and large brown eyes but her clothes were black with dirt, as were her finger-nails and her bare little feet.

'Have an orange.'

'But I'm sick of oranges.'

'There isn't anything else.'

Virgilina Anisetto wraps her jaw against the pain of toothache – a remedy which her grandparents brought from Italy in the last century when they arrived in Brazil to make a new life. But today Virgilina lives with her husband and four children in a hut made of plastic sheets on the grass verge by the side of a modern highway.

Dionise picked up a three-foot machete and, with a sigh, began deftly to cut the skin from one of a pile of bruised, green oranges which lay beneath the table.

'There is a woman up the road who has some orange trees,' said Virgilina. 'She lets us pick the ones that cannot be sold. It is very kind of her. We have very little food. We eat only once a day. We just have cassava root. We never have meat or eggs. We try to grow some vegetables by the roadside, so we get some fresh food occasionally. Once a month I get a kilo of cornflour, of beans and of sugar from a charity. Fortunately none of the children have got seriously ill yet on the diet.'

The family has lived like this for three years, in their plastic hut by the well-maintained tarmac which joins two of the many Brazilian towns where the more fortunate live in conditions comparable to those of Western Europe. But these days there are more and more families by the roadside.

Raga's Story

They built Agus II before Agus I but the order of construction made no difference to Raga Sarib and her father. They lost their land twice over.

The seven Agus projects are hydro-electric schemes all along the Agus river as it plunges from Lake Marawi to the sea on the island of Mindanao in the southern Philippines. Between 1953 and 1985 five of the stations were opened, adding a total of 539 megawatt units to the national electricity grid but at some cost to the local population.

It was in 1975 that Raga's family was first directly affected. The plan was to build Agus II on land belonging to her father Musa and twenty-seven other peasant farmers. The National Power Corporation offered them sixty centavos per square metre. It was not a generous offer. He had a hectare (about 2½ acres) of land and the 6,000 pesos he would have secured would perhaps have been enough to open a small store in the town or buy a pedicab. Like all the other farmers he turned the offer down.

Not long after, all twenty eight men were rounded up by the army and taken to its local headquarters at Tipanoy. There they were stripped of all their clothes and held for three days, without food or water, until they signed agreements to sell their land to the government of Ferdinand Marcos which had recently imposed martial law. Musa signed under duress. But he was so disgusted with the government that he refused to accept the money.

Ten years later Raga was to suffer the same fate. She had married a farmer near the lakeside at Palao-Bubong about ten miles away. Work had been going on for six years to build another hydro-electric plant, Agus I, at the spot where the river left Lake Marawi, to generate a further eighty megawatts. The entrance to the river was deepened and narrowed to increase the flow of water which, over the years, meant that the level of the lake dropped by ten feet. The effects for those who live around the shores have been profound. Fishermen have found that catches have fallen off dramatically. Wide areas of lowland agricultural land dried up as the water table fell. Mosques once sited beside the lake were now hundreds of feet away which meant that, under local Muslim traditions, it was not possible to stay ritually clean on the journey from the place of washing to that of prayer.

'As it dropped we found it more and more difficult to irrigate our crops. Eventually it fell to the point where we could no longer produce rice. I have eight children to feed. We had to abandon the land and, using the little capital we had, come into the city to open a small store. It is not a good life. Before we had our own rice, bananas, coconuts, potatoes, tomatoes and green vegetables. Now we live off only rice and dried salted fish. Our children cannot go to school because we cannot afford it', said Raga.

The story is the same for hundreds of other lake-dwellers and the prospects are even worse. If Agus I begins operation the level of the lake will fall by as much as twenty-seven feet. Thousands of fishermen and farmers will be driven from the land.

Nelson's Story

The seven children had been sent to relatives. Nelson Dutra had no intention of putting up any physical resistance when the police came to throw him out of his home but, he reasoned, anything might happen. It would be best if the children were not there.

Nelson had never expected to find himself in a position like this. He was aged forty-five and had worked all his life as a gardener for the municipal authority and paid his way. He had always lived in rented accommodation because his father had had to sell the family plot to repay his debts to a bank. Sometimes the landlords had not been pleasant people but he had never had any real trouble.

Nelson and his wife Aldinete live in São Paulo, the largest city in Brazil and currently the fastest growing city in the world. Around twelve million people live there and of those some four million live in *cortiços* – grand old houses which have been divided and sub-divided into the tiniest rooms imaginable. They range from the basic to the squalid and the rents charged by the private landlords are often exorbitant. Thanks to Brazil's hyper-inflation, which is calculated monthly rather than annually, rent rises are frequent and large.

'Our rent was 3,600 cruzados a month. It had been that for three months. Then the landlord announced it was to rise to 55,000 a month. I couldn't believe it. My take-home pay was 74,000 a month – that's quite good pay, it's around three times the minimum salary. I went to the legal authorities to see if he could do that. The judge said he could. I offered to pay 20,000 but the judge ordered us to be evicted.

'I spent the notice period looking for somewhere else but it was hopeless. Everyone wanted the same, and worse still they all wanted two months rent in advance.'

Just before the day when the bailiffs were to throw all their furniture out on the street Nelson spotted Jardim da Saúde, an area of waste land on which a few squatters had slashed down the undergrowth and erected shelters of wooden posts covered with plastic sheeting and old corrugated panels. He joined them.

Slowly the occupation grew. When it became apparent that the land belonged to the housing department of São Paulo state, the occupation won the support of a local housing action group which hired lawyers to try to negotiate the right of the squatters to stay. The day I visited the negotiations broke down and the squatters were told that the police would be coming the next day to eject them.

OVERLEAF: *Peasant farmers lost their land for the building of the Agus hydro-electric project in Mindanao in the Philippines. When operations begin the level of Lake Marawi will drop by up to 27 feet. Thousands of fishermen and farmers, who depend on it for irrigation, will be ruined.*

Nelson and Aldinete sat in their crowded little shack surrounded by their belongings – a large wardrobe, an ancient fridge, a battered cooker, a television set, plaster statues of the saints and holy pictures, a pretty little vase stuffed inelegantly with dried flowers.

'If the police come I won't confront them. We will go and find another piece of land to occupy – that's all there is for us to do. I never thought it would come to this.'

Millions of peasant farmers, driven from their land by commercial farming in Brazil, end up in favelas – *shanty towns on the fringes of the big cities. This one in Jardim da Saúde, which means Garden of Health, is in São Paulo, now the fastest growing city in the world.*

Meheret's Story

The garden was the size of a dining table. It was literally no bigger than that. But to Meheret Zere it was the sum of her ambition.

'If only I could have a garden like that,' she said, out loud but half to herself. 'I would grow potatoes and onions, tomatoes and green vegetables. I could have everything I need.'

The garden she was looking at had been built laboriously by hand. Its creator had piled large stones along a little fault-line on the side of the steep hillside in Eritrea to the north of Ethiopia and then heaped topsoil into the crevasses to create a tiny cultivable plot. In it grew five neat rows of a lettuce-like vegetable. The soil on the hill was bone dry but each plant stood in its own island of dampness. The old tin which had been used to water them stood at the side of the little garden, but the nearest water was a tiny trickle, a long climb down at the valley bottom.

Meheret Zere had just arrived at the refugee camp at Filfel in northern Eritrea, free at last from the fighting which had raged all around her for thirty years, on and off – the world's longest civil war which, though she did not know it, was only a month away from ending.

There were 10,400 people in Filfel. All of them had been driven from their land by the fighting and forced into dependence on the food aid which trickled into the area with the volume and reliability of the little river below.

Some had been there for three years. The first had been women and children who had stayed at home to work the fields while their men and older boys went off to the lowlands, as they did for several months every rainy season; only this time the fighting had spread and the men had been taken prisoner by the troops of the Ethiopian government who were fighting the forces of the Eritrean People's Liberation Front which wanted independence.

Meheret Zere had arrived only two months before. She had been in the opposite position when her family was split up – her husband was behind rebel lines and she was trapped on the government side.

'I stayed there and tried to work the land. We managed to save some seeds from last year to plant, but this year there was no rain. None at all. That was what gave me the final courage to do what I had been too afraid to do for five years – cross the front line of the fighting. To get across I had to trick the government troops by telling them that I wanted to go just across the hill to a holy shrine with curative waters – then I just kept on going with my two children.'

In the land through which she travelled the tide of battle had taken a terrible toll. Much agricultural land had been laid waste. But even more good land in areas which the rebels controlled stood idle because farmers had fled fearing the occasional destructive forays the government army made.

Others in the camp told the same stories of marauding troops killing livestock, destroying fields, burning houses, poisoning wells, polluting the grain in their meagre stores and killing or conscripting those who did not flee. Even now the legacy persists; one woman told me, with tears running down her cheeks, of how her twelve-year-old son had recently died after standing on a land mine while herding the goats. The province is full of children who have lost legs or hands in similar incidents in areas where the Ethiopian army littered the ground with the Soviet-made devices.

But Filfel brought some new hope for Meheret Zere. 'Here I want to find my husband, to gather my life together, to build a house and make a garden like this one,' she said.

But it was not a realistic hope for Filfel is a

barren valley in an arid landscape which was chosen for the refugees primarily because it was less vulnerable to air attack from Ethiopian fighter-bombers and near to the supply lines for foreign food aid.

'They have made gardens for themselves,' said Semare Mesfin, the local administrator for the Eritrean Relief Association. 'But they can never be self-sufficient here – for that they must wait until the war is over and they can return to their own land.'

In the huts of Filfel refugee camp in Eritrea to the north of Ethiopia, thousands of women and men wait to be reunited with families divided by 30 years of war. The fighting caused them to abandon their land and scatter in flight. Now they hope to return to their farms.

Alex's Story

Alex Gonzales sat with his elbows on the table in front of him, delicately placed the tips of his fingers together and spoke steadily in soft tones. His manner was that of a young academic. Only his darkened skin gave away the fact that he made his living cutting sugar cane under the burning sun of the lowland plains of the Philippines.

Alex worked on Hacienda Luisita, the sugar plantation which belongs to President Cory Aquino and her brothers and sisters and which is the second biggest agricultural estate in the Philippines. Or to be more precise he had worked there until he was fired for organizing an alternative trades union to fight for the land reform which President Aquino promised before she was elected.

The Hacienda Luisita already had a union, the United Luisita Workers' Union, but Alex and a group of others decided it was too much in the pocket of the management and organized an independent sugar workers' union, Ambalus. Not long afterwards Alex lost his job driving one of the estate's eleven cane-cutting machines.

'That was not all. Threats were made to my relatives saying that they would be penalized. Some, who were casual labourers, found that they were given no work,' he said. 'Others were demoted. My father, Diosdado, had been a farm guard, which is quite a good job on the hacienda; he watched the crops for damage by animals or fire. The job is better paid and not so demanding as that of a labourer. Most importantly it has security because a guard is on the staff and not just a casual worker. Soon after Ambalus began he was demoted to the job of labourer. Such economic harassment is sadly not unusual.

'We set up a team to present the facts to workers at home in the evenings in their *barrios* (villages) on the hacienda. People actually live on the hacienda. There are eleven *barrios* which have been there since the 1920s, though officially everyone there is a squatter. But as soon as we began we were harassed by the Cafgus, a kind of private army of the employers, who prevented us from entering the *barrios*. We had a permit from the local mayor but they said they wouldn't honour it. They pointed rifles at us and snatched our leaflets from us and confiscated our vehicle. Then they sent an armoured car to scare us off.'

All this happened about the time that two trades union organizers from another independent farmworkers' union disappeared in the same town, Tarlac, after being detained by a group of armed men in civilian clothes, one of whom was identified as a sergeant in the local military police. They have never been seen since.

When threats began to be made against Alex, who was by this time working full-time on union affairs while living off the goodwill of his friends, it was decided that it would be safer for Alex to go into hiding. In 1990 alone more than fifty church workers, peasant leaders, and human rights activists vanished in the Philippines, according to Amnesty International, which said that government or government-backed security forces were implicated in the disappearances. Alex did not want to join them. 'I can't live at home anymore. I have to sleep outside the hacienda in a different place each night. It means I have no home now, as well as no land.'

When people have their access to land removed the consequences are severe, that much is clear from the stories of the five women and men above. But it is also clear from their experiences that the whole issue of land is a complex one.

The factors which deny people access to land

are varied. In the case of Virgilina it was the changing agricultural economy of the region; profits were now highest from cattle so the land was turned over to ranches and the day labourers were sent packing. For Meheret the cause was devastatingly simple – war. For Nelson it was the exponential growth of the population of a big city – a problem which is replicated all over the Third World as the world population grows and as more people leave the rural areas and migrate to the city. For Raga it was a classic development conflict between the needs of the national economy (as perceived by the central government) and the disruption caused to a local population which pays the price of the grandiose development project – the island of Mindanao with its agriculture, forestry, fishing and gold provides sixty per cent of the government's earnings but receives only fifteen per cent of government expenditure. For Alex the problem was the basic economic structure which condemns large numbers of people to a form of wage slavery and which responds all too often with violence when challenged.

The list could continue. A Bangladeshi peasant who inherited only a handkerchief of land when his father's tiny plot was divided among his sons. A farmer from Mali whose fields turned to desert with the constant encroachment of the Sahara. And there are millions more who have land and skill but not enough resources to make a living.

What then should be the response of those who live comfortably in the Western world

Inside one of the long dark dormitories on the Hacienda Luisita sugar plantation, owned by Cory Aquino's family. Each houses around 200 sacadas – seasonal labourers with no land of their own, who migrate around the Philippines looking for cane-cutting work.

but whose consciences are pricked by such situations? Most of us look for an aid agency to support. So how do they respond?

In emergencies, agencies send out food aid but common sense soon dictates that this alone is an insufficient reaction. Long-term development is needed to prevent the emergencies from arising – the philosophy is summed up in the Chinese proverb: Give a man a fish and you feed him for a day, teach him to fish and you feed him for life. Such an approach may well be appropriate to the problems of Meheret in Eritrea. The immediate problems caused by war and drought can be eased by sending food aid. Further progress can be made by an integrated development programme which establishes education and health care alongside projects to promote water conservation and combat soil erosion.

But there is a further stage in the process. Those involved in development work begin to realize that, for the poor, all too often the goalposts are moved. The fishpond installed by an agency dries up because it was badly built by foreign engineers out to make a quick buck from the construction. Or the pool is polluted by unregulated industry discharging waste upstream. Or the site is stolen by a rich land-grabber and his gunmen.

Slowly there comes the realization that in many cases basic economic and social relationships need changing. How does a development agency cope with this? One agency, Christian Aid, offered to show me in an extended tour of countries in the three continents in which it works.

The problems are myriad, as we will discover in the chapters which follow. Some of them are international – the imbalanced nature of international trade and the burden of Third World debt. Others are governed by national policies – the concentration upon cash crops in countries which do not grow enough food for their people. Others are at a commercial level – the erosion of good ecological practice by the profit-motive. Yet others are social – the lack of participation in decision-making by women, who do most of the work in the Third World. Together they add up to the enormous handicap under which the world's poor labours. But at the base of it all is the issue of land. For without land, and the means to make it productive, the poor will never begin to take control of their own destiny.

2 | Squatters in their own Land
The eviction of the tribal peoples

If there was a moon I could not see it, for the cloud hung like a mist over the mountain top. It had been dark when I arrived and I had not seen the face of my guide. He led the way up a steep slope of crumbling soil which broke up underfoot as we clambered higher. It was a disquieting climb for I knew that there was a 1,000-foot drop beneath me. Maybe, then, I was disorientated by the time I reached the top. Or perhaps the sight below really was unearthly.

Lines of lights were set in a vast and curious pattern across the face of the hillside opposite and in the valley between. Many of them were moving in slow diagonals up and down the side of the hill. Occasionally an arc of brilliant white light would burn incandescently on the lower slopes or on the valley floor, briefly illuminating clouds of pink smoke. From the whole alien complex came a low throaty hum. It was as if I had stumbled across some gigantic beast from another world at slumber, around whose back fluttered thousands of tiny fireflies.

I was in the Cordillera mountain range in the north of the Philippines looking down on a gigantic opencast mine which operates, such is the hunger for gold, twenty-four hours a day. The man who had brought me there to see it was an Igorot, a member of one of the groups of indigenous people in the region. His ancestors had hunted and farmed these lands for thousands of years before the arrival of the mining company which owned the sprawling Antamok site below.

Or at least the members of the interna-tional mining consortium said they owned it. Certainly they could produce land titles going back to the colonial period when the United States seized control of the islands from the original colonizing power, Spain. But this, to the Igorots – who number more than a million people, three-quarters of whom live below the government's poverty line – did not constitute ownership. I was face to face not just with one of the world's biggest opencast gold mines, but with one of the classic questions in the subject of people's access to land: What is ownership and how is it to be established?

But this was not the moment to raise such abstract points. The Igorot group had decided to kill a chicken in honour of their visitor in the traditional manner. 'This is the way in which we kill a chicken for a sacrifice. It is called *pinik pikan*,' explained the man who had led me up the mountain, Rudy Pudsoc, a member of the Kankana-ey community which occupied a tiny village near the peak of the ridge.

The chicken was held upside down and killed with a series of sharp taps to its head with a stick. After its feathers had been burned off it was cut open and its innards inspected. 'It is a good omen,' said Rudy, pointing inside the bird. 'See, the gall bladder is full and it is covered by the liver – your visit here will be safe and prosperous.' As the chicken was being cooked, with garlic and ginger, the Kankana-ey spoke of how their life had changed. The pressure cooker in which the chicken was cooking was evidence enough that it had.

'The gold has been here since the time of Kabunain, the god who long ago brought customs and laws to our people. In those times the gold could be picked like fruit from the trees. But our people violated the laws so Kabunain was angry. He banished the fruit from the branches and drove the gold into the roots of the tree. Since that time men and women have had to dig for the gold. But the gold was given in the first place to the Igorot people, not to outsiders,' said Rudy.

How far back could he trace his family's occupation of land in this area? I asked. As a title deed the legend would not stand up to the scrutiny of a court of law.

'Perhaps not in your Western court but before the court of the elders of an Igorot tribe it would,' he countered sharply. 'And who is to judge whether your system is superior to ours? Yours holds sway only because you have accumulated wealth and power behind it.'

Rudy's wife Balen laughed. She was a small woman; her facial features were clearly Igorot but they were not so broad or flat as those of her husband. 'He does not like your question because he did not live here until he married me. He is a Bontoc, a war-like people from the Mountain Province further north. But my father farmed and mined here. So did my grandfather who was here in 1903 when the Americans came and first opened the big mine. My people have been here for hundreds of years.'

Things had changed slowly she said. The native peoples who dug for gold in tiny pocket mines cut by hand into the hillside were pushed off the land as the company's gigantic earth cutters devoured more and more of the area. Some were given jobs in the deep mine shafts which the company also sank into the mountains, but most jobs had gone to outsiders who were brought in and crammed into huge bunkhouses on the valley floor.

'The main problem it has caused is that the big mine has altered the water table so that the springs which once fed our land have all dried up. There are many places we cannot farm. Even drinking water is in short supply. The spring at the bottom of our hill used to gush freely; now you have to stand for thirty minutes to fill a five-gallon container. We have had to ration every household to two gallons a day and when we want to do any washing we have to hire a jeepney [a uniquely Filipino vehicle, a cross between a bus and a lorry] to take a thirty-minute ride to the river.

'The other big problem is pollution. The dust from the surface mining rises in the air and gets everywhere. The rivers are tainted with the chemicals they use to extract the gold. The small miners just use borax but the big mine uses mercury and cyanide. The tailings from it have caused animals to die around the river and rice paddies to be poisoned.'

Balen's neighbour, Lourdes Ayadi, used to work in the local health centre. 'That was fifteen years ago and we had none of the problems which we have now – coughs, fever, TB, asthma, stomach ulcers . . . It has got worse since they opened a processing plant which gives off fumes that the wind carries here. We don't know what is in them but we can feel their effect. People here used to live until they were ninety, now they die twenty years earlier, of diseases like cancer which were rare before.'

The next morning the full scale of the Benguet Corporation's mining activity was revealed. As

PREVIOUS PAGE: *Dawn over the opencast gold mine of the Benguet Corporation at Antamok in the Philippines. The land once belonged to the Igorots, the native inhabitants, but they have no pieces of paper to prove the ownership of their ancestors.*

dawn broke there could be seen down the near side of the valley dozens of individual pocket miners moving haphazardly, at different paces, down the precipitous slopes of scree and vegetation to the little scars on the hillside which marked the entrances to their individual tunnels. On the far side, in dramatic contrast, huge lorries and bulldozers moved in relentless patterns across a devastated landscape of blasted rock and dusty earth. The dust was everywhere in the valley, coating everything with a fine white film. Above the pit could be seen the abandoned rice paddies which were now without water.

'The mountain is like a woman,' said Rudy, looking down on the mine which exploits 440 separate veins of gold, 'and these machines are like men who violate her. Where they have stopped the grass does not grow again, even after years.'

His own mine was a different thing altogether. I crossed the mountain and descended on the other side, out of sight of the Antamok operation, to find it. The path zig-zagged perilously down the sides of a plunging wooded gorge to a small clearing at the edge of which was a small opening in the rock about half the size of a kitchen door. Inside it was about 150 feet long, cut through damp clay of distinct brown and grey strata. The roof was supported by pit props made of pine from the surrounding forest. From them hung fungi of orange, pink and white in exotic shapes. At the face, a tomb of black clay glistened with pyrites and specks of gold.

'We mine in the dry season and then process it in the rainy season when there is plenty of water,' said Balen, vigorously brushing the mud from her hair with her hand as we left the tunnel. 'In the past we were mainly farmers. We planted rice and kept livestock. The women made brushes from tiger grass to sell in the market. Mining was a supplement to our income. But since the water has dried up we have to mine far more.

On the fringes of the massive commercial mine at Antamok the tribal people continue to tunnel for gold in tiny hand-dug pocket mines as their forebears have done for centuries.

Now even the women do it. We tried alternative agricultural techniques; we planted mulberry trees to cultivate silkworms but the dust killed them all. The trouble with mining is that it is a bit of a gamble. You can make some money, but other times you get nothing at all.'

The women are miners too at the community of First Gate, which takes its name from its proximity to the first of a series of security gates the road passes through on the way to the Benguet Corporation's big mine at Antamok. I had hoped to visit it to ask the management about the Kankana-eys' complaints and to compare the living and working conditions there with those of the indigenous people outside. But I was turned away at the main gate by uniformed security men. On the way back I stopped at First Gate and climbed from the road up the mountainside to the village perched at the top.

'We are lucky that our pocket mine is on the other side,' said Balen. 'There we get no visitors.'

The visitors to whom she referred were the Antamok security men who had been causing problems for the pocket miners of First Gate. Six months before the company had suddenly fenced off a new area which it had decided would be the next area to be exploited. The security men had told the inhabitants, members of the Kiangan tribe of the Ifugao people, that they could no longer work their pocket mines there.

'At first we ignored them,' said Bernard Boligon, whose father migrated to the village from the Ifugao homeland further north to find work before Bernard was born. 'Then they arrested nine of us and took us to the police. Some, including me, escaped. But the others had to pay fines, plus bribes to get out.

'So then we went back to work, but we camouflaged the entrances to the tunnels after we had entered, so they couldn't see us. It was hot inside and we were afraid we might suffocate but we managed for a while. Then one day they heard us and they shouted that they were going to blast the tunnel and that we could come out if we wanted to. When we came out they dynamited it. On other occasions they smoked people out and beat them up afterwards.'

'That was when we got involved,' said his wife, Helen. 'We thought they wouldn't blow up the tunnels if women were in them so we took over the mining. For a while nothing happened. Then early one morning four security guards came. We were just carrying up to the road the ore we had dug over the past three weeks. There were 200 sacks from ten separate mines. They ripped open every sack and spilled the ore down the steep valley side where it could never be recovered. Since then we mine only at night and in a different place each time. We call it hit and run mining. Whatever the company does we will not give up, for if we do not mine we do not eat.'

But the story of the Igorot groups around Benguet has not been entirely one of setbacks and defeats. Early in 1990 when the corporation tried to reopen an old pit off the main valley the groups got together with the help of the Cordillera Resource Centre for Indigenous Peoples' Rights, which is funded by Christian Aid, and barricaded the road for several days, forcing the company to abandon its plan. Since then lawyers of the corporation have been to negotiate with the Igorot leaders, offering a new road and measures to combat the dust and the water shortage in return for co-operation in reopening the old mine. The Igorots voted to reject the offer.

Back in the capital, Manila, I contacted the headquarters of the Benguet Corporation, also known as the BCI, which is the biggest producer of gold in Asia. It is expected to make $28 million this year from Antamok alone. An affable lawyer in its legal department sighed when I put the Igorot complaints to her.

'We do our best to avoid confrontation but the legal position is quite clear. We have titles to the land which were issued under the US regime in 1902,' said Attorney Soledad de Castro. 'The people who are causing all the problems are not in any case the indigenous people.

'The land originally belonged to the Ibaloi tribal grouping who were farmers. Most of these people acknowledge that their ancestors sold the land for cash to the Americans when mining began. They are still there on the land and we have an agreement with them that, although legally they are squatters, they can stay there until we need to develop that part of the land. When that happens we pay them compensation for their homes and any improvements they have made, for their crops and small mines – but

Inside a pocket mine two Igorot miners tug out a barrow full of ore. Gold could once be picked from the trees, according to their tribal lore, until an angry god drove it through the roots of the trees into the earth.

not for the land because that is ours anyway. The company has agreed to provide schools, water systems and new roads, and ninety Igorot families have recently signed an agreement accepting that.

'The ones who are refusing are not Ibalois. They are migrants to the area, Kankana-eys who are not too friendly to the Ibalois. They are squatters who have come since 1903 and who try to take advantage of us by mining on the edges of our operation. We're not very happy about that. But in the interests of good relations we don't make any distinction between them and those who are indigenous to the area. We offer them the same deal. We hope that local government officials will be able to persuade them to co-operate.'

In terms of the present constitution and laws of the Philippines it was clear that the Igorots were on a losing wicket. But, as Rudy Pudsoc had pointed out, the Western system of jurisprudence was not the only code of law which covered property ownership. I decided to find out more about Igorot law and discover a place where it was in daily use.

It takes twenty-two hours to drive from Manila, north to the Mountain Province, and then into the remote area in which the village of Mainit hides in the folds of the deep highland valleys. It was almost dusk as I arrived, far later than expected, and an evening mist was falling down from the hilltops. It seemed to be moving through the village like a living creature, lingering over some of the roofs and swirling through the stilts on which the houses were raised. It was only when I reached the streams which ran through the centre of the village that I realized it was steam.

'Do not touch the water. And do not go near to the edge. The ground looks firm but it is marshy below the crust which the heat has baked,' warned the Bontoc who had guided me along the long winding trail to the village. 'A visitor here sank in recently. Her leg was cooked. They tried to carry her to hospital on a stretcher. But she died on the way.'

I picked my way gingerly across the stones and little planks of wood which had been laid across the bubbling stream of water which seemed in places to rise, boiling, from the earth. 'We cannot build a bridge because the waters change their course constantly.'

Night in the tropics falls suddenly. It was already too dark to see anything by the time I had finished negotiating the delta of steaming rivulets which guarded the top end of the village where the most senior of the village elders lived. I sat in the darkness and waited for him on the raised porch outside his substantial wooden house.

The chief elder arrived and introduced himself. 'My Catholic name is Andrés. My Igorot name is Tafaling,' he said as if to underscore from the outset the cultural ambivalence which has become part of modern Igorot life; the peoples who were categorized by the American colonists as 'non-Christian peoples' have by and large succumbed to conversion this century. His hair was white but his face had the strong features of a man in the prime of life. He was aged fifty-five, he said. 'An elder is not the oldest person in the village but the oldest one who knows most about tribal law. But before we can talk it is necessary that you must first eat and drink. Custom requires it.'

The Philippine army was sent to the valleys of the Mountain Province, like this one at Bontoc, but failed to quell resistance to hydro-electric schemes flooding the valleys. Eventually the plans were dropped.

All present ate from a large communal bowl of sticky rice flavoured with a stew of pork. His wife served glasses of *bayas*, a wine made from sugar cane, which tasted strong, like Japanese *sake*. Only then did he speak: 'The ownership of land is not proved by a mere piece of paper but by the knowledge of the whole community. That is our tradition which goes back to the forefathers who have tilled the land since before tools were made of iron. Each one passes the land he has tilled to his children. There are three classifications of land: rice terraces, grazing and forest.

'The rice terraces go to the eldest; if they were inherited by the father they will go to the eldest son, if they were inherited by the mother, to the eldest daughter. Younger children have to go elsewhere to find their living or else work as labourers for the eldest. He may, if he wants, give them a share, but they may not ask. You can only ask a kinsman for land if the hot spring has come and taken over your land, which is a sign, we believe, that someone will die there soon.

'Personal goods are inherited in the same way – the most valuable of these are the *sangli*, Chinese jars which are the family heirlooms of the Bontocs, centuries old. The house always goes to the eldest daughter when she marries; until then all the children can continue living there. The widow or widower has to move out then too, to live with the youngest child.

'Grazing land is shared by all the family who have the right to graze their animals there. The livestock is shared among them. Pastoral land can only be cultivated if the council of elders approves.

'Forest is owned by the community. Everyone can take firewood but not cut timber for sale unless they are going to clear the land to make a farm, which the elders must approve. They adjudicate on all land matters. Only last month we had before us a man who had moved a *tambak*, that is a boundary stone, by six inches. Only two cans of rice could have been harvested from the area he gained. But the land is a most sacred thing and cannot be violated in that way. He was fined by having publicly to cook and serve food – the food he hoped to gain – to the elders.'

The council is exercised by the need for appropriate punishment. Recently one man, who had been drinking, committed a murder. 'The decision of the elders was that the relatives of the dead man should hold down the murderer and stab him through the heart with the same single blow, so there should be no blood debt among the descendants.'

The laws on land and violence have been thrown into sharp focus in Mainit recently for gold has been discovered there. 'You may visit the mines tomorrow,' the headman pronounced.

The next day the whole village rose at dawn to immerse themselves naked in a series of pools into which the hot springs had been diverted at various points down the valley to produce a succession of hot baths of varying temperatures – the hottest for the men and the coolest for the children. All were too hot for me. 'That is a sign that the water does not like you,' said one old bather, gravely.

Over breakfast the villager in whose house I had stayed took me aside to confide: 'Having some gold is a good thing. We can enjoy life now. We have enough food at last. We even have chicken and San Miguel [the local beer]. We have wood to build new houses and money for clothes for the children. Things improved after we discovered the first gold in 1974: before that we had no clothes, only G-strings; we had no corrugated iron for roofs, only straw; we had no enamel plates, only wooden ones. But now too much gold has arrived. The children will not go to school; they will not work in the fields. They spend all day at the mines. They are spoiled. They do not care about the old ways. You will find no hospitality there. You will see.'

This latest find of gold was by a river, about forty minutes walk away along the narrow walls which divided the rice paddies where the newly transplanted seedlings were growing strongly above the water. It was the children who had first spotted the sparkling yellow flecks in the soil of the riverbed and began panning for gold. Impressed with what they brought home the adults joined in. A year later they had moved slowly upstream and then begun tunnelling into the side of the mountain where the rock was soft and no dynamite was needed.

The entrances to the tunnels were disguised. The word was that the Mainit-Bontoc were getting a kilo of gold a month out of the mountain. The market value of that was around $10,000 a month. They were afraid of thieves as well as the surveyors of the Benguet Corporation who

Hot springs bubble from the ground in the village of Mainit, in the Mountain Province of the Philippines. But gold has been found near the village, and now a monthly income of around £5,000 threatens to alter the traditional ways of the Mainit Bontoc Tribal group.

had already made several forays into the area.

Some months before, one villager, named Piley, had decided that there was a quicker way to raise money than by mining. He had done a deal to sell part of the land to the Benguet Corporation. But when the BCI engineers arrived with their survey equipment the Mainit villagers had held a meeting and then confronted them. Some engineers left peacefully. Others continued working and had been driven out.

'There are many ways of driving people out,' the headman had said. 'Our women can bare their breasts, as was done in another village recently. It is shameful for a Filipino man to see a woman's nakedness so the engineers had to leave. But if the BCI insist on returning other groups will come in, with arms.'

His veiled reference was to the guerrillas of the New People's Army (NPA), the armed wing of the Philippine Communist Party, which has one of its strongholds in the Cordillera mountains. It was a threat which was reiterated more boldly at the villagers' gold mines.

When I arrived at the rough campsite, which had no fewer than fourteen processing mills, I approached one miner, who had seen me with the village elders the night before. 'We have more than twenty tunnels. It is very easy mining. Most of them are only twenty feet long,' he said.

He had only begun speaking when another miner approached. 'Why are you telling an outsider this?' he asked. Turning to me he said: 'You are not welcome here, whatever the village elders say. You should know that if anyone comes to take our gold this will become a battleground. There have been centuries of war here and the people always win because of the terrain. All invaders have found this: first the Spaniards, then the Americans, then the troops of Marcos. No-one here will speak to you. Leave now.'

Back in the town of Bontoc, the provincial capital, Victor Ananayo, a welfare officer for the Episcopal Diocese of the Northern Philippines, explained the miners' hostility. 'The problem has its roots in the Regalian doctrine inherited from the Spanish. This declared that all land and natural resources belonged to the king. As a result this government considers the region and its natural resources are its to dispose of as it wants.'

The Spanish colonizers refused to grant land titles to Igorots. And when the Americans took over they based their land law on Spanish precedents on the grounds that the Igorots were considered incapable of grasping the significance of land ownership. As a result more than one million native people were omitted from the land register thus rendering them invisible or even non-existent in official eyes. In 1903 the US colonial power made a law declaring that all decisions by the 'chiefs of the non-Christian tribes' were to be considered 'illegal, void and of no effect'. From that point the Igorots became squatters in their own land.

During the colonial period any other individuals could lay claim to any piece of land by making a sealed bid, which contained at the least twenty-five per cent of the amount offered for the land. Those people already on the land were not even informed, unless they could read the notices published in English and Spanish in Manila.

The injustice of the whole business was later acknowledged by the US Supreme Court when it condemned the system for its 'ceremonies of which presumably a large part of the inhabitants had never heard'. The land which was sold, the court acknowledged, was land which the Igorots 'by native custom and by long association – one of the profoundest factors in human thought – regarded as their own'.

But successive Philippine governments found it convenient to continue with the old colonial formula. It was reconfirmed in 1974 when President Ferdinand Marcos, under martial law, issued the Ancestral Land Decree which gave Igorot groups ten years to establish a title to their lands before they were 'declared open for allocation to other discerning applicants'.

The year after, Presidential Decree Number 705 announced that all land on a slope of more than eighteen degrees (which was most of the Cordillera area) was a forestry reserve. Under this law no-one is allowed to live, farm, graze animals, hunt or cut wood in the area.

'This contradicted the indigenous concepts of land ownership. But Marcos wanted to build a series of hydro-electric dams along the Chico River,' said Victor Ananayo. 'It would have made 100,000 Igorots homeless and destroyed their homes, rice fields and ancestral burial grounds.'

The decree was a cover for Marcos to give logging concessions to his cronies. This was at a point when sixty-one per cent of Philippine forests had already been destroyed in the preceding two decades and the livelihood of the Igorots had already been severely affected. Those who depended on traditional hunting and gathering or clear-and-burn agriculture lost the forests which were their homes. Those who relied on more settled agriculture found productivity drop as a result of the accelerated erosion and silting from the deforested watersheds.

Sympathetic lawyers offered to act for them, free of charge. But the Igorot elders refused on the grounds that their participation would give credibility to proceedings which would inevitably be decided in favour of the government. There was a series of meetings and mass actions to stop the work on the dams. The government brought in the military. That was when the armed struggle began.

But there are also organizations which support the fight for Igorot rights by unarmed methods. One of the key bodies is the Cordillera Resource Centre for Indigenous Peoples' Rights (CRC). 'It was founded in 1981 in response to the spontaneous protests against the plans to flood huge areas of the region,' said Geraldine Fiagoy, an Igorot who was a university lecturer in anthropology before becoming the centre's director. 'People were resisting in defence of their ancestral lands, and were then accused of being subversives and supporters of the NPA. Many people were detained in the years 1976–81 and many others were killed. Others were tortured and many Igorot villages were strafed and bombed.

'Originally we saw the promotion of indigenous people's rights as part of a wider human rights campaign after the abuses under martial law. Our main concerns were human rights, giving paralegal training to community leaders, organizing the students and getting wider publicity for what was going on. We were talking to them about things like not signing anything they were given: people who couldn't read had been signing deeds of sale. But gradually we widened our brief to cover general Igorot issues, in particular the issue of land rights, and research on the treatment of the environment in the region.'

Out of the movement has since grown the Cordillera People's Alliance, a grouping of 120 local groups which are campaigning for regional autonomy, the recognition of ancestral land holdings and the mineral rights to them, the payment of compensation for past injustices and the withdrawal of all troops, together with the disarming of all paramilitary units in the region.

OVERLEAF: *The fields around Mainit are passed from one generation to the next by a complex pattern of tribal tradition. But can such oral laws prove a match for the lawyers hired by mining companies to stake claims?*

Victor Ananayo is convinced that such organizations are the only way for the people of the Cordillera to maintain a grip on their land and to recover control of the environment in the region. 'People have tried their best to work within the law to promote indigenous rights but the response of the government and Congress has been very discouraging. So we now have to rely on ourselves and strengthen our organizations to assert our rights. You can't stop change but you can develop some degree of control.'

The old woman was aged 142, they said. She had been found living wild in the jungle and was the only one left who could speak the language properly. But it might be difficult to reach her, for she lived in the heart of the reservation in an area from which the Indians had never been driven, not in all the 500 years since the Portuguese had first set foot on the eastern coast of Brazil. The story turned out to be half true.

I had arrived in Brazil to look at the work of an organization named CIMI which was set up by the National Catholic Brazilian Bishops' Conference to help the Indian peoples resist further encroachments on their lands. It is the main agency through which Christian Aid supports the attempts of the Brazilian indigenous peoples to organize themselves. CIMI was set up because the Indians were dissatisfied with the official national Indian protection agency, Funai. After a decade of frustrating dealings with the body, many Indians concluded that the Brazilian government sees Funai's real role as managing the sale of mining rights on Indian land and even assisting landowners who want to evict the original occupants to clear forest and open up land for ranching. CIMI tries to help the Indians to make use of such law as does exist to assert their rights to what is left of their traditional environment.

One of the tribal groups which was experiencing particular difficulties at the time of my visit was the Pataxó Hãhãhãi of the Pau Brasil region of the state of Bahia. The landscape of their Paraguacu-Karamarou reservation came as a surprise; it was not rainforest but cleared, undulating, rough pastureland broken only by the occasional tree or patch of undergrowth.

It gave enough cover, however, for the man with the bow and arrow to appear in my path without warning. He was a disconcerting figure with broad facial features and a powerful torso. He wore a singlet and shorts but in his hair was a wicker headband and at his throat hung a necklace of large teeth strung together with reed beads. He held the bow, untensed but at chest height, and walked silently towards me. For a moment there was something menacing about his advance but then he lowered the weapon and slowly raised his left hand in greeting. His name, he said, speaking in Portuguese, was Aruana.

In the village a group of women and children had assembled to greet me. In a thatched hut whose sides were open to the air they began to chant and dance in a circle as I approached. They were an odd sight. They wore skirts of grass and wicker headbands decorated with pink and blue feathers. On their faces, arms and chests they sported red war paint. But between, incongruously, they all wore cheap embroidered blouses or printed T-shirts of the style sold in nearby towns. A few minutes later Aruana appeared, now also wearing a skirt of grass and wicker armbands to match his

In Brazil the original inhabitants cling to the ways of their forebears. But this bowman from the Pataxó Hãhãhãi Indians shoots only to preserve local tradition. Commercial loggers and cattle ranchers have destroyed the forest and the animals his people used to hunt.

headgear. Behind him were other men, some of them similarly attired.

The face paint was traditionally only worn at times of sorrow, a young chieftain, Aka, explained. There were three main shapes: 'a cross to represent the joining of the dead ancestors with the living Pataxó; a circle to symbolize the union of people and the continuity of life; and a bow and arrow to show our willingness to suffer in the battle to come.'

The song, Aruana explained, was about a plant from the forest which produced a traditional drink used in celebrations. But the plant no longer flourished because the forests had all been cleared by the white men. So much was no longer available – the animal whose teeth he wore around his neck, which he described as an antelope with a nose like an elephant, had gone too. The men produced examples of their weaponry and laid them ceremoniously at my feet: elaborately carved spears, lances bound in sisal, long arrows with feathers beautifully curved along their shafts. The older ones were made of dark, heavy wood; the newer ones were altogether lighter. The supply of traditional wood has gone, one man explained. The women and children began another dance and the men joined the circle.

But as I watched all this a sense grew in my mind that there was something peculiar about the whole proceedings. The war paint was applied with a red felt-tip pen. On the table was a Thermos flask. One of the babies had a plastic dummy in its mouth. Aka, beneath a resplendent headdress of blue and brown feathers, wore jeans and flip-flops. Though the younger men and women introduced themselves by Indian names, the older folk all had names which sounded Portuguese. Against this background the official proceedings had about them a self-conscious, anomalous feeling of the kind which characterizes tourist exhibitions of native dances in the

foyers of Sheraton hotels throughout the world.

And so it transpired.

Almost the entire Pataxó Hãhãhãi people had been driven from their 36,000 hectare reservation in the 1950s by land-grabbers who had the backing of the state governor. Those who would not leave were killed. Officials of the Indian protection agency had connived in the process after being bribed. The Pataxó were dispersed through the region, with a few of them returning quietly to accept jobs as day labourers for the new landowners. In the process they learned the language of the conqueror and forgot their mother tongue.

It was a story which echoed the sad saga of the disintegration of so many native peoples throughout the Americas. What made the story of the Pataxó Hãhãhãi different was that in 1975 a European anthropologist arrived to make a record of their culture before it disappeared. The meetings organized to prompt collective recollection reawakened the sense of communal identity of people who had had no contact with one another for almost thirty years.

In 1982 the rejuvenated tribe invaded the reservation and occupied 1,200 hectares of it. For the next three years they cut themselves off from all avoidable contact with the outside world.

'We had lost our language. The older people had hung on to most of our traditions but the young people had grown up without a proper sense of them. We wanted to re-establish our tribal identity as well as making ourselves agriculturally self-sufficient', said Aka.

Older members of the community helped the young to reconstruct. Arida Pataxó who is aged fifty was a key figure. 'I was born and grew up here until I was twelve. At that time the gunmen were sent to get my father because he would not sell his land. He said he would never part with the land of his ancestors. So they came for him. He fled into the forest. It was all forest here then.

Several others were killed. I escaped with my aunt. We came back three years later and all the forest was gone. We got a job working for the land-grabber. We were day labourers for him for twenty-six years until we seized the land back.

'When we retook possession the young people had to be taught many things. I taught them how to make the traditional clothes. I taught them which feathers to wear for feasts and which to wear for times of struggle. I had to teach them about the plants and flowers – which are to be used to make drinks, and which for herbal medicines. I had to teach them the songs and the dances that go with them. Many of them are in the Pataxó language. I don't understand it properly now but I can still remember the words of the songs and incantations.'

The response of some of the ranchers has been

War paint is defiantly applied by the Pataxó to mark their determination in the battle to regain their ancestral reservation. But the natural dyes of the region were lost when the forests were cleared. Instead they use felt-tip pens.

violent. There are a total of 398 ranchers who claim they now own the 36,000 hectares of the reservation. All are threatened by the legal action which the Pataxó Hãhãhãi have now filed with the help of CIMI; many had been in the process of filing to acquire official titles to the disputed land. Some have responded with the violence which is traditional in rural Brazil.

Gunmen, sometimes arriving with the local police, regularly harass the Indians. Aruana's father, Antonio Julio Pataxó, was one of eight Indians who went out carrying bows and arrows to defend their land against ten gunmen armed with heavy calibre rifles. 'They opened fire on us as we came out of the forest. We had no cover. We didn't have a chance,' said one of those present. 'There were ten *pistoleros* and they had the military police backing them up. Antonio was hit. The gunmen came back the next day but the federal police had been called in and so the *pistoleros* backed off.'

Antonio Julio was hit in the head and para-lysed down one side. He lay in bed before me, his muscles wasted and his stare vacant, as the story was told. He has been bedridden for six years. Others were not so lucky. Eight Pataxó have been killed by gunmen since the occupation. One of the Indians, taken by gunmen while farming his plot, was found mutilated – his finger nails had been drawn out, as had a number of his teeth, and he had been scalped and castrated.

'They said they did it because he was a snake,' one frightened young Indian told me. 'That is what they call us. They hiss it at us in the street when we take our produce to town. They say

After their land was stolen the Pataxó went to town to find jobs and adopted Portuguese customs and clothing. Some stick to these. But others are determined to re-assert their Indian identity and have returned to traditional garb.

we are not human, that we are snakes, because snakes are the lowest form of life.'

The struggle for recognition of their rights will be an uphill one for the Pataxó Hãhãhãi. In 1988 the Brazilian government issued a new list of indigenous peoples and their reservations. The Pataxó Hãhãhãi found that they had been left off. 'They say we are not an indigenous people but that we are a colonized people because we trade with outside groups, because we have some inter-marriage and because we do not speak our own language,' said Aka. Suddenly the motive for that slightly sad pantomime of cultural rediscovery was evident. The remaking of themselves as Pataxó was not a free-spirited action so much as a desperate attempt to assert their right to land.

'There is only the Old Woman left who speaks Pataxó properly. That is why we are trying to get people to learn it from her, but it is difficult because she does not speak Portuguese and she lives so far away. But she is our last chance. We have to get it from her and systematize the language so we can all learn it again.'

The Old Woman was to be found in a distant corner of the reservation, in an area which had been the personal fiefdom of an official of the forerunner of Funai and which had, therefore, remained undisturbed. It took another day's journey to get there.

It was dark when I left the village and a misty dawn was breaking as I arrived at the outpost where the Old Woman lived. There were only two families there. 'We are the Hãhãhãi, not

Pataxó Hãhãhãi. We are the descendants of the last of the really wild Indians,' said Katiku Hãhãhãi, who lived there with his brother. 'I have lived here all my life. There have always been Hãhãhãi living here in this place.

'My father, Natchiko, was one of the wild Indians who were caught in 1928. They were brought here to tame them. They fastened them to trees or locked them inside buildings until they were domesticated. They kept them like that for six years then they made them learn cultivation. Some of them could not adapt to life outside the forest and soon died. Only a few had children. Some of them lived a long time. The chief lived until he was seventy-six and only died because he was bitten by a snake in the fields over there. That was thirteen years ago. Now they are all dead, all except the Old Woman. She has no relatives so she lives here with us.'

He went to fetch her. Baretta Hãhãhãi was a shrunken little figure with a face which looked as if its ancient features had somehow collapsed in on themselves like the oral civilization of which she was now sole custodian. She wore an old striped sweat-shirt over a thin floral frock and had an old nylon sweater pulled around her shoulders against the morning cold. She stood silent as he spoke.

'She speaks only Pataxó. She speaks a bit of Portuguese that no-one can understand. She can understand us but we can't understand her. My brother and I can speak a bit of Pataxó, enough to have a bit of a conversation with her. An anthropologist came from São Paulo to try to get down a systematized version of the language. But when she showed me what she had done it was all wrong. She left a tape-recorder and when there is no-one around we sometimes ask her questions to get her voice on record. But she won't speak when there are other people around.'

The Pataxó language is almost dead. All the tribe speak Portuguese except for this old woman, Baretta Hãhãhãi, who is said to be aged 142. She is the last survivor of a group captured in the forest in 1928. She is the last Pataxó speaker. The others are desperately trying to relearn their language from her.

FACING PAGE: *Aruana Pataxó sits on his father's bed and tells the story of the old man's paralysis. The gunmen of a rich man had arrived to chase the Pataxó from their land. The old man had gone out to confront them with his bow and arrow. They shot him with heavy calibre rifles. He has been bedridden ever since.*

What had she said about the old life? 'Before they died she used to talk to the others about the old times: how they hunted, how they travelled through the forest like nomads, roaming from deep inside to as far as Ilheus on the coast. She talks often about *iriyami carcachinga*, a form of cassava that they used to cultivate in the forest. It won't grow anymore, now the forest has gone.

'She says they used to wear skirts made from certain parts of the undergrowth; apart from that, and the rings around the arms, they were completely naked. They lived in groups of about twenty families and the leader of each group was called the Ronhakay. She says: "From the outset the whites attacked us. We had been a big people, with many groups in many places over a large area, but slowly they killed us off. Now," she says, "I am the only one left."

'She says it was a good life. Everyone rested, everyone fed. No-one got bored. Here people get bored, she says. Life is dreary.'

The Old Woman stood, chewing her cheeks, and looked at the visitors as Katiku spoke.

'Sometimes at night, when she is sad, she cries that she wants to go back to the forest, even now. We do not really know how old she is. An anthropologist came six years ago and worked out that she was 136, so that would make her 142 now. I don't think that can be right. But she was an old woman when she came out of the forest in 1928, so they said. I think she is probably 120, but there is no way of knowing.'

In Brazil there are two categories of Indians – Colonized and Indigenous. Because they speak Portuguese and trade with non-Indians, the Pataxó Hãhãhãi have just been reclassified by the government as Colonized. Therefore they lose their reservation. Can they win their fight to overturn the decision?

Suddenly the Old Woman spoke. Katiku looked surprised. 'What is she saying?' I asked.

Katiku smiled. 'She is asking if you will give her a lift into town in your vehicle.'

The Old Woman spoke again. 'She is asking if you will buy her a pair of sandals.'

I said I would.

'She says she wants yellow sandals. They have to be yellow, to match her best dress.'

The last hope of the Pataxó Hãhãhãi climbed into the car and headed for town.

3 | Plantations and Ranches
The landless fight back in Brazil

'Yes, I set fire to people's houses.' Joaquim Lopez was matter-of-fact as he made the confession.

'Yes, I pull them down. Why shouldn't I when they are built illegally on my land?' His voice was calm and steady.

'Yes, I take armed men with me to do it. Yes, I carry a gun myself. It is necessary for self-protection. These are dangerous people.'

It was not the kind of blunt admission which might have been expected from a rural landowner in Brazil. But then Joaquim Lopez looked an unlikely representative of the Brazilian ruling class. He arrived at his fairly small-scale sawmill in Bahia province in an old white saloon car, wearing a red sports shirt and light brown slacks. He looked slightly overweight, but no more than the average European. He wore a gold watch, but it was not a Rolex.

Somehow I had expected him to be richer and less willing to discuss his techniques for ousting peasants from the surrounding land. Brazil is the fifth biggest country in the world – it covers about half of the entire area of Latin America but has a population of only 141 million. Yet despite the fact that it has huge areas of underdeveloped land it is riven with violent conflicts between the eleven million landless peasant families and the big landowners. The landowners, known as *fazenderos*, constitute only two per cent of the population but between them own seventy per cent of the land, much of which is not farmed but held as an investment. Every year more and more land comes into the ownership of this elite and the number of landless farmers grows.

Brazilian land law is complex. It is possible for the rich to buy large tracts of land from the state government irrespective of who lives and works on it. But, under a law designed to increase national output, it is also possible for a landless family to occupy and cultivate land which is not being properly used. Once they have been there for a year they cannot be evicted until a long judicial process is complete. Under it a ruling must be made on whether the land which has been occupied falls within the law which enables the government to expropriate land and reallocate the title to the new occupants.

That, at any rate, is the theory. In 1990 and 1991 about 230,000 families received land in this way. But, in practice, in many remote country areas the law is actually made through the barrel of a gun. Landowners all too often hire gunmen to drive the peasants off the land or kill them – thousands have died in a process to which, according to Amnesty International, the Brazilian authorities turn a blind eye.

Joaquim Lopez acknowledged that there were many landowners like that but insisted that he had killed nobody. It was not difficult to believe him.

The kind of landowner, or land-grabber as the peasants often describe them, who did behave with that ruthlessness would probably not bother to give an interview to deny the fact to a visiting journalist. Further to the north, in one of the ranch areas bordering on the Amazon which is a notoriously more violent region, the hired

thugs of one *fazendero* had tried to kill a BBC journalist only weeks before – he had escaped only because the assassin's gun jammed.

But we are leaping ahead. In between the ousting of the tribal peoples from their land, which we encountered in the last chapter, and the development of such head-on conflicts between the *fazenderos* and the landless peasants there are a number of other stages which must be considered.

The roots of the problem lie in the structures bequeathed to Brazil, as to so much of the Third World, by the process of colonialism. To the European imperial powers the huge expanses of land in Latin America and Africa were nothing more than farmlands to produce foods and raw materials for consumption in Europe. The Portuguese Crown was no exception. Its policy towards Brazil was to make large land grants to colonizers as a reward for military and political services rendered or to prospective export crop producers. By contrast to the development of the United States, where the strong homesteading tradition of the small pioneer farmer fostered the growth of democracy and individual land-holding, in Brazil the colonizers' approach gave rise to oligarchy and huge sugar, coffee and cocoa plantations with massive areas given over to little but the raising of beef for export. Their descendants still own it today.

To provide labour for the colonial enterprise some five million black men and women were captured in Africa and brought as slaves to Brazil, with one million of them said to have died on the voyage across the Atlantic. Slavery was abolished in Brazil in 1888 but a visit to a cocoa plantation there today makes the visitor wonder how much really has changed.

By dawn the women and men were already waiting with expressionless faces, their shoulders huddled against the chill morning mist, at the doors of the administration block at the cocoa plantation known as the Fazenda Agua Branca outside the town of Wenceslau Guimarães in the middle of Bahia. The economy of the state is seventy per cent dependent upon the crop from which chocolate is made and which most of its people have never tasted. Minutes later they were tramping up the mud paths between the cocoa trees, carrying their lunch in small bundles of cloth or old plastic sacks, to the place where they would squat for eight hours splitting cocoa pods.

The workers sat in pairs, one man and one woman, at either end of a small barrow next to an enormous pile of the pods which they had picked the day before. The man sliced open one of the yellow pods, each about the size of his hand, and the woman scooped the sticky white fleshy beans from the pod and into the barrow. They worked so quickly that their fingers seemed just a blur. (Sometimes, I was told, a worker would slice off one of his fingers – an accident which previously would have earned compensation, but the *fazenderos* had recently abolished the practice, claiming that workers were cutting off their fingers deliberately.) From there the beans would be carried down the hill in panniers on a donkey and then fermented and dried on beds above stoves on which other workers had to walk in bare feet at temperatures of 120 degrees Fahrenheit to rake the beans.

The plantation was not the orderly rows of

Workers on a cocoa plantation in Bahia, Brazil, use long-handled blades to slice cocoa pods from the trees. The price of cocoa has dropped by two thirds since 1985. Today more than half the area's workforce is unemployed. The extensive plantations mean there is no other land for them to use to grow food.

bushes I had expected. The cocoa pods were picked from trees some twenty feet high which grew over a huge area apparently at random with patches of periwinkles and curling ferns growing amid the debris of last year's leaves. Apart from the humidity and the temperature, which by mid-morning was in the nineties, it was rather like walking in an English beech wood. One of the women waited until I had wandered off on my own, away from the estate officials who accompanied us.

She brushed her way through the undergrowth carrying a machete with which she lanced stray pods and tossed them into the basket over her shoulder. She glanced around to make sure that the *fazenda* administrator was not watching and then said to me: 'Raise the minimum wage.'

Her name was Maria, let us call her that, for she was anxious not to be identified. She thought I was a buyer from one of the multinational cocoa-processing firms which are the influential middlemen in the international chocolate industry. 'Raise the minimum wage. We work hard here, but we do not get enough to live off. We get some wage rises but the price rises are always more and faster. I have nine small children to feed. They are not getting enough to eat. My husband is ill and cannot work. I cannot afford the medicine for him.'

Wages in the cocoa plantations have fallen in recent years. At the time of my visit workers earned, on average, only two thirds of what the Brazilian government decreed to be the national minimum wage which is itself, in real terms, worth less now than at any time since it was introduced in 1940. Working conditions had deteriorated too. Employers now routinely denied workers a national insurance card (to avoid the employer's contribution); they refused to pay the holiday pay or the annual bonus which was legally compulsory. Many routinely

sacked all workers after eighty-nine days, and then re-employed them after a few days' gap, because certain statutory rights applied after ninety days. Others imposed new conditions on workers, only taking on women who could produce a doctor's letter to show they had been sterilized or requiring all employees to sign an undated resignation letter so that they could be dismissed without payment or complications whenever the estate required. The alternative was all too clear – 225,000 of the area's 350,000 cocoa workers were currently unemployed.

The cause of all this is a fall in the international price of cocoa which has put sixty-five per cent of the region's 350,000 cocoa workers out of a job as the plantation owners try to maintain their profit-margins. Cocoa is today only a third of the price it was on the international markets in 1985. The Western multinational firms encouraged the planting of huge estates in Malaysia and Indonesia, despite the fact that West Africa and Brazil already produced enough to satisfy world demand which is at a stable level. As a result a massive stockpile of cocoa has been built up – equal to forty-four per cent of the world's annual production – which allows the cartel of buyers to fix increasingly low prices.

Maria's face was drawn with anxiety, partly no doubt because of the situation she was describing, but partly because she was afraid she would lose her job for speaking out.

She stood before me, pleading with a subdued urgency. It was as if she stood there on behalf of all those without land, forced by the logic of the economic formula which the West has handed to the developing nations into a kind of wage slavery.

It was Maria who was condemned to carry the burden of decades of unfair trade in which the industrial nations sell expensive services at high prices to developing countries and, in return, pay the lowest price they can fix for Third World raw materials.

It was Maria's nine children who were going hungry because Brazil cannot afford to grow food on its rich agricultural land; instead it must grow cash crops to export, to earn the dollars it needs to pay off its share of the Third World debt – a debt accumulated through the high interest rates of ideological monetarists in the Reagan/Thatcher era, through the reckless behaviour of Western banks, and through the irresponsibility and greed of too many of the leaders of the world's poorest peoples. So in a land of plenty Maria was doomed to watch her children slowly develop the chronic malnutrition which would gnaw at their stomachs, stunt their growth and retard their mental development.

Is slavery too strong a term for this? Maria was entrapped. There was no other job for her. The conditions and wages were broadly similar on

Eight workers but only two wages. The slump in the cocoa industry has allowed owners to introduce new systems of piecework. So workers bring their families with them to earn what previously one man earned alone. Even the children work for 11 hours every day.

plantations throughout the area. And no matter how hard Maria worked, she would never earn enough to sustain a decent life for herself and her children.

Indeed the existing system is actually increasing landlessness. Those peasant farmers who did own land on which they produced some cocoa on a small scale, along with a few subsistence crops, have increasingly found that they cannot make ends meet. Gildasio Marques da Assuncão was typical of many: 'Five years ago when the price of cocoa was better we could survive by working our own land. Now we have to look for work on a plantation as well to supplement our income. Each year we have to work more hours outside.'

Each year more and more of those small pro-

The pods are sliced open to extract the beans. Before if a worker sliced off a finger or thumb compensation was paid. Now the owners have abolished the system – they claimed that workers used to cut off their fingers deliberately.

ducers get into financial difficulties and end up selling their land to the big estates which use the land more intensively and with much higher levels of environmentally damaging agro-chemicals, according to Luis Carlos, an official of the Polo Sindical, an organization which Christian Aid is funding in its attempts to support an emerging regional cocoa workers' union among these desperately poor people. It will help to organize those who work on plantations to campaign for fairer wages. It will also help small producers to market their wares. Generally small producers produce better cocoa. It is grown organically or with minimal use of pesticides because the peasants are too poor to afford the chemicals, and the traditional drying and maturing process they use produces a higher quality bean than the accelerated artificial processes of the big producers. But the international buyers prefer bulk to quality so a co-operative system to market the smaller harvests is needed.

'Do people earn enough? The truth should be told – they do not,' said the surprisingly frank administrator at Fazenda Agua Branca, Pedro da Silva Agevedo. 'But I do not fix the pay rates. The *padrão* (owner) fixes the rate on each *fazenda*. Unfortunately some pay less than is due. That is why we have introduced the *empreita* system.'

That night outside the plantation other workers felt able to talk openly about the growing problems of recent years and about the recently introduced *empreita* system. 'First the number of jobs was cut. A *fazenda* which five years ago employed fifty people will now employ only ten,' explained Luis Carlos. 'They have done it by sub-contracting sections of the *fazenda* out to particular workers who get a set amount and employ other workers where they need to. So a man will go there very early in the morning and take all his family with him, children too. And everyone will work hard all day. At the end of the

day the man may get a little more than he would have under the old system of daily hire. But he has worked harder, for fourteen hours instead of eight, and the employer has got all his family's labour for free.'

There are some workers who are not unhappy with the change. Balbino das Nevis, who has been a cocoa worker for twenty-five years, said: 'On balance it's been better for me. I can earn 5,000 cruzados a week where I would have earned 3,000 before. That's good because I have eight children to feed. I pay those who work for me about the same as they would have got on daily hire. But it's much harder work, so I only hire the hardest workers.'

But most, like Ramiro José Fagunha, with twenty-one years in cocoa work, are discontented. 'I also took on a contract but I'm much worse off,' he said, 'I could only do well if I exploited the people who work for me. And as two of my employees are my wife and my aunt there's not much point in that. The only advantage of the system for me is that I can guarantee jobs to members of my family.'

With no land of their own to fall back upon the only option for those who are unemployed is to live off relatives or leave the area. 'Many have gone. There is a bus every day which goes to São Paulo. People sell their TV set to get the fare. Sometimes they write to say they have got a job and things are going well. Others write to say it is terrible and discourage others from following; they say they would come back but they can't raise the bus fare. Some we never hear of again,' said Adeilton da Silva, who lost his job recently after eighteen years in the industry which he joined as a boy of nine. 'I was sacked for refusing to sign one of the blank resignation letters. There is nothing to keep me here now. I think I might go to São Paulo. I know it is a risk but I think I will go and take my chance.'

There is one other option for those left without

work or land in the countryside – to seize land for themselves from the huge tracts which the rich have grabbed and are not using. It is a high risk strategy.

The crack of a single shot floated eerily in the air across the valley. The women of Verdum settlement looked up anxiously. Without a word being said they shared the same thought. How stupid it had been to fix on a shot as the signal for a successful operation. How could they now be sure that it had gone according to plan? What if the shot had not been from their men but the enemy? What if one of their men was now dead?

On the surface it was just an ordinary Friday afternoon. Men had been working in the fields. Two of the older boys, riding bareback, were rounding up the few animals the village owned. In the puddles and patches of sticky and slippery mud which last night's torrential rain had created on the bare earth between the houses, smaller children played. Inside the make-shift houses – hastily assembled from panels of woven bamboo, black plastic sheeting and rusted old corrugated iron – the women were working over the ornate old floral-fronted enamelled stoves their grandmothers had handed down to them. The evening meal they were preparing was of rice, vegetables and flour mixed with palm oil.

But an hour before a group of six men from Verdum had ventured up to the hilltop. Their

PREVIOUS PAGE: *In many parts of Brazil groups of workers occupy unused land on big estates and begin to farm it for themselves. This group at Vitória, in Paraná, occupied the land six years ago and each year harvest a good crop of maize.*

objective was to ambush the gunmen who had been terrorizing the village for more than four months, firing randomly at men working in the field, at visitors and even at children on their way to school.

When the shot was heard the women left their kitchens and hurried outside to peer apprehensively up into the hillside forest and to the grain silo beyond, where the gunmen had made their base. In a panic the remaining men of the village rushed into their houses and emerged with a motley collection of old Winchester rifles and obsolete carbines. Without waiting they set off in four or five separate groups to join their fellows on the hilltop. The women hushed the children, who had begun to gambol and chatter with the excitement, and turned their faces to the hillside to wait nervously for the sound of more gunfire.

Verdum was an hour's drive from the town of Cascavel in the southern state of Paraná on the borders with Argentina and Paraguay. It was one of 6,000 settlements which have been established in Brazil in the past six years by landless peasants who have simply moved on to idle land, erected houses and begun to farm. Some 95,000 families have been involved in the process, much of which has been organized by a movement for the landless, Sem Terra, another of the agencies with which Christian Aid has established a partnership in its mission to find ways of helping the poor to strengthen their position. A total of 4.5 million hectares has been taken over and measures have been implemented there to improve agricultural techniques and establish effective marketing systems.

'The land occupations really began in about 1985 when a number of factors combined. Mechanization of farming meant that the amount of work for landless labourers decreased. High interest rates meant that a lot of small farmers went bankrupt and had to sell their land to the big

landowners. Then the building of the big hydro-electric schemes at Itaipu and Segredo flooded a lot of good farmland which was heavily populated. More than 100,000 people were displaced. Yet at the same time huge areas of land were standing idle,' said Seno Staats, who took part in one of the first successful land occupations at nearby Vitória six years before. The occupation has since been validated by the Brazilian courts which have granted land titles to the peasant farmers. Seno is now the regional co-ordinator in Paraná for Sem Terra. 'The national constitution states that land is eligible for redistribution if it is not being put to productive use. All we are asking is that the law of the land be applied.

'This part of Brazil had really only been opened up in the 1960s. Much of the land which had been claimed had been used only for

Brazilian land law allows the state to expropriate land which is not used productively. Occupation by peasants can force the authorities to begin the expropriation process. Sometimes the courts rule in favour of the occupied and allow them to keep it, as happened at Vitória.

Until seven years ago Maria de Andrade and her husband were landless labourers. The children often went hungry. Since they occupied the empty land at Vitória things have got better each year. Maria, now one of the community leaders, still worries about poor education and health care. But at least there is always plenty of food on the table.

logging out the temperate hardwoods and then abandoned or left with a few cattle dotted on it. It was this land which Sem Terra began to take over. We did our homework first. We found out who owned the land and what his title was – in about sixty per cent of the cases we found it was dodgy anyway, it had been obtained through falsification or bribery. In some instances the land had been stolen from small farmers by land-grabbers who used gunmen to oust the original inhabitants to turn the land into rangeland for cattle. The gunmen were not local; they were brought in from Matto Grosso or even from Paraguay.'

The response to land occupations by the poor has, all too often, been to bring in the gunmen once again. Such was the case at Verdum.

The leader of the community, Solange Czycza, recalled the whole perturbing process. Her Christian name was Italian and her married name Polish, for like most Brazilians in the southern states she was of European stock. The others at Verdum had a mixture of Ukrainian, Lithuanian, Swiss, Greek, and German names, though most of them now had lost the languages which their grandfathers had spoken. 'Fifty families had occupied this land in 1988 but were evicted by the police the next year. Many people were injured and the leaders had to go into hiding. Two years later we decided to occupy again because the land had still been left idle in the interim and the state had a new governor who seemed against allowing the police to be used to evict people.'

'Before we came here we were involved in another occupation but the land was poor and there were too many families', said another of the community leaders, Valdemar Trachez. 'We were often hungry. Sometimes we did not eat for three or four days in a row. At the worst point we had eighteen people die of starvation. It was grim, seeing a child die of hunger and not being able to do anything about it.'

'The other reason we wanted to branch out on our own was that at the other place everyone involved in the occupation was trying to make it on an individual basis,' said Solange. 'Getting land is not enough. Just because you get a bit of land doesn't mean that you will progress or improve your living conditions. We see small producers going under and losing their land all the time. Much more is needed. That is why we are interested in exploring the idea of working the land as a co-operative.

'It brings obvious advantages in terms of making better use of our resources. Together we can afford to hire a tractor, which singly we cannot. It enables us to buy in bulk for both our domestic and farming needs. But it will also help us to market our own produce in bulk and cut out the middlemen. Working collectively will give us more chance of getting access to government services, including credit. It will give us a much greater chance of getting a decent road, and water and electricity laid on, and health and education services provided. It will free up individuals to work in other areas – the landless movement, politics or education.'

They arrived at Verdum in the dark and rain early one Sunday morning in 1989. 'We unloaded our belongings from the lorry in which all seventy of us had arrived and began to build our houses,' said Solange. 'For a month we cleared the land. We clubbed together and hired a tractor to do the worst parts. When we ran out of food some of the local churches fed us. Then we began to plant.

'The initial threat from the *fazendero* was delivered by his foreman: we would be allowed to clear and sow but we would never harvest. At first the *fazendero* tried to get a legal order to evict us but he failed. Then representatives from the government's land ministry came and made a field inspection and declared that the land did qualify for expropriation. That was when the gunmen began to appear.

'Four months ago they began to let off shots close to the village. Then they intimidated our men working in the field. Then they shot at a lorry we had hired to take our maize to market. Then they shot at the children.'

One of the Verdum residents, Ledumira Portela, is a teacher in the local school. Every day she walked there with schoolchildren from the settlement. 'We had to walk past their base. Then one day a fusillade of shots came from there at us. We heard them whistling through the branches above us and hitting the trees around. The children were terrified. I had to pretend to be strong and tell the children that there was no danger, they were only trying to frighten us. But

it was an awful experience. The children did not sleep that night. None of us went to school for two weeks.'

Soon afterwards the *pistoleros* lay in wait for her son Alessandri, a cherubic little blond-haired boy aged six. They told him that soon he would be an orphan. His mother and father would be killed and he would be left alone.

Eventually the men and women of Verdum decided they could tolerate the situation no longer. 'We had 290 hectares of the estate. The gunmen were camped on the remaining ten hectares, by the grain silo which the *fazendero* had built – the only thing he had done to improve the property . . .' said Solange.

'He has planted not one inch,' said Valdemar.

'. . . We decided that so long as they were there we would never have a moment's peace. We decided we had to drive them off. To confront them now was the lesser evil.'

The original plan was to confront the *pistoleros* with a large crowd of people and use sheer numbers to drive them off. The day I arrived at Verdum settlers from two previous occupations, at Vitória and Ibema, had been due to join in the attempt to oust the gunmen. They had not turned up. A tense meeting of the Verdum settlers was held in the open area between their huts.

'Well, it looks as if the rain has prevented the reinforcements from getting here,' Solange told the assembled villagers. 'So what shall we do?'

An animated debate ensued in which almost everyone participated.

PREVIOUS PAGE: *The land occupation at Verdum, in Paraná, Brazil, is only a few months old and permanent houses have not been built. The settlers still live in huts of plastic and reeds. But they have grand plans for a co-operative with a tractor, fishponds and a beef herd with their own abattoir.*

'There are just about enough of us to drive them out,' said one settler.

'We might have enough people to confront them and drive them out,' said another. 'But we don't have enough to hold the place and at the same time to come down here, as we'd planned, to dismantle the village and move it up to the silo site.'

'We should go up on our own and then send for the reinforcements.'

'What if they don't come? They don't seem very enthusiastic. Once they've got their own land they don't seem interested in helping us.'

'We should put it off until we know the others will come.'

'If we do that news is bound to leak out and the *fazendero* will have the chance to reinforce with more gunmen. Then we'll never get them out.'

'What do the other women think?'

'We're fed up of hanging around, living with all our things packed in boxes and sacks, waiting for the move.'

'We should go now. If we can surprise them there won't be a shoot-out.'

'They don't take their guns when they go for water. We could ambush them, capture the place, call the press and put them on show with their guns.'

'Let's do it.'

So they voted and the ambush party was sent up the hill.

In the event it was a failure, though not as dramatic as the women had feared as they gazed up the hillside after that single shot. The search parties came back in dribs and drabs, flushed and breathless. Finally the ambush group returned. All talked animatedly, trying to piece together what had happened. There had been three *pistoleros*, not two, it turned out. The third one had not seen the ambushers but he had spotted their tracks and fired that single shot to alert his fellows. Solange, Valdemar and the

other leaders of the village went into a conclave which lasted all evening.

Next morning, an hour before dawn, the settlers picked their way through the mud in the darkness to assemble in the largest of the village's huts. Their faces were dour and their mood bleak. They sat in two groups, the women around the stove, the men on benches around the room rolling cigarettes or passing around a bowl of maté, a powdery green tea. Solange sat chewing at her fingernails. One of the committee, Sebastian, whose job in the community is to look after their few dairy cattle, spoke: 'We had a meeting last night and decided that if the people from Ibema came in the night then we would march up and make up a mass occupation; if they didn't we would have this meeting to decide what to do . . .'

The flag of the movement of landless peasants, Sem Terra, has many uses. Behind it the people of Verdum marched to claim unused land for themselves. Now it serves as a curtain to the doorway in one of their temporary huts.

'To see how brave people were feeling,' said Valdemar.

'. . . It doesn't look good. It's almost dawn. So what do people feel we should do?'

The men and women sat and looked at one another. Smoke rose in blue clouds around those with cigarettes. Most people sat and looked at the floor. One or two others glanced around the group, waiting to see who would speak first. Sebastian's wife, Sueli, stifled a yawn. Solange inspected her bitten finger-ends.

'What a silence!' said Valdemar grimly.

Eventually someone spoke. 'We blew it yesterday. They'll be on their guard now.' The discussion began. The factors raised were much the same as the previous day, only now the tone was far more subdued. The eventual conclusion was different too.

'We must wait for the others to arrive – that was our plan yesterday and it should be the same today.'

'I'm worried about the lack of support from the other settlements. If they won't come to help take it, they won't come to help defend it later. We said that all settlements would have the use of the silo after we had taken it but still they have not bothered to come.'

Slowly the group began to work itself into a mood of indignation. How could they do it without others? Where were the other settlements? Where were the regional executive of Sem Terra? OK, so it was raining, but even if they couldn't get a large number of people down they could have sent someone to indicate what was happening.

The mood of the meeting is grim. For months gunmen, sent by the nominal owner of the land, have harassed them. But now they have begun to shoot at children of the settlers on their way to school.

Sebastian spoke: 'Let's hear from those who have not spoken.'

'I think we should wait.'

'Yes, we should wait.'

'Wait. It's not our fault if the others won't come to support us. We can't be expected to do it alone. We don't have enough people. We must get on to the regional level people and tell them to get organized.'

Downcast, everyone acceded to the consensus which had emerged. Solange rose to fill the kettle. The meeting began to break up. As one man opened the door everybody stopped. Through the open doorway they could hear the growing noise of a lorry coming down the valley. The people from Ibema had arrived. The occupation was on. Later that day the gunmen fled as the silo was taken by force of numbers.

It is difficult to get to meet the *fazenderos* who constitute the other side in these disputes. Many of them are absentee landlords, living among their wealthy friends in the well-to-do suburbs of Rio de Janeiro. Others, like the owner of the estate at Verdum, also have huge ranches in Paraguay where they spend much of their time. Joaquim Lopez was an exception, perhaps, because he was a fairly small-scale landowner with two estates, one of them a cocoa plantation and the other a tract of virgin Atlantic rainforest which provided the timber for his two small sawmills in Bahia in north-eastern Brazil. Perhaps it was because, although prepared to resort to violence to drive peasant families from the land, he was not prepared to kill, as so many landowners in Brazil do, apparently without a thought.

Sunset at Verdum. A first attempt to evict the gunmen failed. Later the settlers succeeded in removing the gunmen. No one was hurt.

Our first contact with Joaquim Lopez was indirect. Just near the village of Utumuju is a small area of forest which is the home to twenty-two families whose forebears have lived in the area for at least three generations but whom the landowner says are squatters.

The first house stood at the top of a hill at the end of a dirt track an hour's laborious drive from the main road. The forest had been cleared by burning and the small fresh green shoots of cassava plants could be seen pushing their way through the ashes – traditionally the first stage of cultivation after the removal of the rainforest. Just before the building a group of peasants were engaged in felling trees and levering them across a wide area of the track. The barricade was to deter the *fazendero* or the police officers he had recently sent into the estate.

The three nearest houses had recently been attacked by Joaquim Lopez and his men. One was just a shell of blackened posts where a house had been set on fire. Another was a heap of broken tiles, severed posts and crushed mud and sticks which had once been wattle and daub walls; pieces of clothing and old kitchen utensils could be seen buried in the debris where the house had been pulled down with all its contents inside. The third was still standing, despite the fact that all of its main posts and lintels had been sliced through with a chain saw.

'The saw broke down before they had finished. They tried to carry on with a machete but the building was too solid for that,' said Francisco Cruz, the occupant of the house. 'They did it on election day, while we were all away at the polling station.'

He and his fellows had gathered to recount the chronicle of the woes they had suffered at the hands of Joaquim Lopez. They spoke of stands of hundreds of their banana trees being bulldozed, of crops razed where they grew, of produce stolen on its way to market. One woman, still clearly disturbed two months after the event, told of how she collapsed with shock when a gang of *pistoleros* had shot into the ground at the threshold of her home where her small children had gathered around her skirts in fear. A man spoke of how he had been forced at gunpoint to assist in the demolition of his own house: 'They wouldn't let us take anything out. Everything was destroyed inside. As my wife stood crying amid the ruins we were told that if we built it again we would die.'

Joaquim Lopez was unrepentant. 'Look at it from my point of view. My family began to buy land around here in 1908. It was acquired from the state of Bahia by my grandfather. The entire area was forest then and he used oxen to pull timber from the forest and then floated it downriver. He built sawmills and a hydro-electric scheme to power them which was nationalized in 1960 and taken into the national grid. I am telling you all this so that you can see that we are not newly-arrived adventurers. After my grandfather the estate was managed by my father and then my uncle. I was living in Rio, working as an engineer, when in 1983 I got a call to say that our land had been occupied. So I packed up my job and came out here to take over the management from my uncle who couldn't cope with the situation.

'At first the occupation was a disorganized affair, with odd individuals just moving into the forest and clearing a bit of land for themselves. I initiated action which got rid of these people. But two years later the land was occupied in an organized way, backed up with the legal advice. A group of local landowners got together and

Joaquim Lopez, the landowner, in his timber yard. 'Yes, I set fire to people's houses,' he says. 'Yes, I pull them down. Why shouldn't I when they are built illegally on my land? But I do all I can to avoid confrontation and killing.'

FACING PAGE: *At Utumuju in Bahia, in north-east Brazil, peasants have been ousted from the land farmed by their parents and grandparents. They have occupied a stretch of Atlantic rainforest which was being kept as a timber reserve by a big landowner. They have cleared it and planted banana trees.*

decided that, as a gesture of good will and to short-circuit the legal process, we would each give ten per cent of our land to the commission to be given to local landless people. We gave 1,000 hectares in total. But it soon became clear that our gesture only served to encourage other squatters. More came, and many of them were not local people. Many were not wanting to farm, they were just clearing my land of timber and selling it themselves.

'We bought the land to farm the timber. It wasn't just an idle investment. The land which the squatters claim is "unproductive" was in fact a timber reserve for the sawmill business. That is not unproductive in my eyes; it is part of the business. Then squatters occupied part of the land which I was gradually expanding to become a cocoa plantation. I went to court to get them evicted and got a judgement in my favour but the state governor [who was a political opponent] refused to send in the police to enforce it.

'So what option do I have? Yes, I set fire to people's houses. Yes, I pull them down. Why shouldn't I when they are built illegally on my land? Yes, I take armed men with me to do it. Yes, I carry a gun myself. It is necessary for self-protection. These are dangerous people. But I do all I can to avoid confrontation and killing. That is why I go to pull down the houses when I know there will be no-one there. Some I know are empty all the time; they are not proper houses, just shacks of four posts and some plastic sheeting, just erected so that the squatter can say in court that he has a house on the land. Others, which I know are occupied, I have my men watch so that we can destroy them when there is no-one there.

'I know that from a foreigner's point of view

After a visit by a gang of gunmen the villagers of Utumuju decide to construct a barricade before the first of their scattered houses.

Houses are cut down with chainsaws and weeping families evicted. But normal life also goes on. Children play in a stream by a burned-out house.

one side must be in the right in this situation and it is easy to have sympathy with the peasant. But in fact the situation is more complicated. A lot of blame must be put at the door of the government. They make laws and then do not enforce them. If they want to expropriate my land, fair enough. But let them get on with it, and come up with some money to compensate me. As it is there are these occupations and then the legal process drags on for ten or twenty years. I get no money and I can't get on with developing my land. So I lose both ways. If I could I'd get out. Land in Brazil these days is just one big headache.'

Estacio Alejandré Cruz would agree. Estacio is Francisco's father. He is aged eighty-one and was born on the *fazenda* and still lives there in a tiny hut perched amid the trees high on a steep and inaccessible hillside.

'Nothing has changed,' Estacio said. 'We had all these problems with his grandfather, Joaquim Lopez Marques. We used to farm quietly and then he would come along with his gunmen and say that the land was his and we would have to move. He would say we could move to another area of virgin forest. But after a few years, when we had cleared it and we had planted cocoa trees which had begun to produce, as well as our subsistence crops, he would come along and take that too. I made and lost three farms. So did my brother. But what could we do? He had the money and the gunmen; he once nearly killed my brother when he protested.

'All of this is wrong. He said he had land titles. Who can say? None of us could read. In any case justice is not a matter of pieces of paper. Justice is about everybody having enough food to eat. In the old days we just managed. We cleared new land and it provided us with enough to eat. We had enough that my wife never needed to work for anyone; that is my proud boast. But today there is not enough food. People do not have enough to eat.

'I think that justice should rule. God gave the land for everyone. How can one man own the land? The land is here forever, but the life of man is short. It is the land which owns the man, not the other way around. You are born from the earth and you return to the earth. The only part of the earth you can ever really own is the seven palms in which you are buried. [In rural Brazil the traditional burial plot is seven palms deep].

'When I was a boy my grandfather used to say that by the year 1990 all lands would be liberated. That would be God's blessing. But around here there is no blessing on the earth. It is a cursed land.' He spat on the ground. 'But you must drink some coconut juice before you leave . . .'

4 | Working through the Law

How the landlords ruined land reform in the Philippines

She arrived in a cavalcade of army jeeps and bullet-proof limousines surrounded by military outriders. Thousands of soldiers, some in gaudy dress uniforms, others in combat fatigues, stood to attention. As she alighted a twenty-one-gun salute was fired.

Corazon Cojuangco Aquino had been President of the Philippines for almost exactly five years and she looked happy and relaxed amid the trappings of presidential power as she arrived at Manila's Fort Bonifacio to celebrate Filipino National Army Day. A military band played and she marched in perfect step with her generals, her arm crooked in a fixed marionette salute as she inspected the assembled troops and the neatly aligned rows of tanks, armoured cars and motorized guns behind them.

It was an occasion heavy with irony. She wore a bright yellow dress – the colour worn by her supporters on the day of that euphoric demonstration in 1986 when more than half a million women, men and children flooded the streets of Manila and People Power blocked the progress of columns of tanks and troop carriers trying to keep the dictator Ferdinand Marcos in power.

In those days she had been elected, as the widow of Marcos's murdered chief rival, Ninoy Aquino, on the promise of a better life for the ordinary people. Cory, as she was universally known, pledged an end to human rights violations and the reform of the army. She offered a programme of social justice which included more jobs and improved education, health care and housing. She guaranteed equal rights for neglected minorities like Muslim and tribal Filipinos. She undertook the 'repeal of repressive laws and dismantling of economic structures which keep workers in a state of quasi-slavery'. She pledged an end to the fighting and a ceasefire with the rebels after which she would 'enter into a dialogue with the insurgents in order to afford the new administration the opportunity to redress their legitimate grievances'. She also promised land reform.

Five years on she had arrived to celebrate the foundation day of that same army which her supporters had stopped. It was an army whose members still retained immunity from prosecution over the disappearances of church workers, peasant leaders, and human rights activists, some fifty of whom vanished in 1990, according to Amnesty International. It was an army which was still supported by groups of government-armed vigilantes; the private armies of plantation owners which had terrorized the population in the Marcos years were abolished under Aquino reforms but in 1989, under pressure from her generals, she allowed their reformation under a different name.

Much had changed in the five years since the promise was made. As I arrived in the Philippines the demonstrators were once more on the street, but their slogans were now directed against Mrs Aquino. The woman who once marched with them now looked more at home with the military. In her speech to the army that day she pronounced that her generals' strategy of 'total war' against the rebels of the New People's

Army (which involves the devastation of whole regions of the country where the rebels have their base, laying waste the land, crops and homes of thousands of innocent farming families) might well be the army's 'crowning achievement' in its ninety-four-year history.

Sister Christine Tan was one of those 'ordinary people' who put Cory Aquino in power. From an upper-class Filipino family, like that of Mrs Aquino herself, she was once the head of her religious order, the Sisters of the Good Shepherd, in Manila. Twelve years ago, however, she abandoned her elevated position and went to live with the poor in the slums of Metro Manila.

OVERLEAF: *Harvesting the sugar cane on Hacienda Luisita, the estate of the family of Cory Aquino in the Philippines. Almost 25,000 workers and their children live in villages on the hacienda and have no land of their own. In her election campaign Mrs Aquino promised them land reform.*

Lorries stacked with sugar cane wait for milling at the hacienda sugar factory. By the time that her land reform law was passed landowners had ensured it was peppered with loopholes. Now they can, legally, avoid giving land to peasants as pledged. Instead they turn the land into a limited company and issue shares to the labourers.

One of a series of mills which crush the juice from sugar cane. Loopholes inserted in the law exempt such machinery from the land reform process. Crops in the fields, irrigation systems and much else are also exempt. Clever accounting means that – instead of receiving land – each worker now receives a payment of less than £1 a month. The result is called land reform.

What she found there was tens of thousands of the poorest people in the land, most of whom had fled from the countryside where land or jobs had become impossible to find. They had flocked to the capital in the blind hope of a better life. They ended up in a sink of desperation where squalor, disease and crime were the norms of everyday life.

'They were living like pigs,' said Sister Christine, a keen-eyed woman in her early sixties, who has no sentimentality about the simplicity of poverty. She settled in one of the slums and began a threefold programme, supported in its infant days by Christian Aid, which combined bible classes with welfare improvements and education courses.

Twelve years later her approach had produced real change. The people of the slums had acquired a new sense of self-confidence and control over their own destiny. In the neighbourhood there were now seventy groups each centred around a bible class. Between them they had developed mechanisms for taking on the corruption and inefficiency of local government. After an eighteen-month battle with the authorities they obtained a clean water supply for the area. Other small but vital improvements followed. They themselves built 380 toilets in the community. They developed housing associations, employment co-operatives including their own soap factory and job training schemes to free local people from the bondage of exploitative landlords, sweatshop employers and the desperation of crime (which had fallen off considerably in the area).

It was from communities like this that the support for the People Power revolution came. These were the people who responded to the call by the country's leading cleric, Cardinal Jaime Sin, that his flock should jam the highways of the capital to prevent Marcos's troops from crushing the fledgling government of Cory Aquino. The sheer weight of human bodies brought the army to a halt. Tanks ground to a standstill in front of nuns who knelt in prayer before them.

But five years on all this goodwill for Cory had evaporated. Sister Christine, a personal friend of Cory Aquino's, and who was appointed by her to be a member of the commission to oversee the new constitution after the fall of Marcos, pronounced that Mrs Aquino had failed utterly. 'It's too late now. We've missed our chance in history. We had our golden opportunity and we did not seize it. Cory has been a great disappointment.'

The Hacienda Luisita is a vast sugar plantation, the second largest land-holding in the Philippines. It is owned by President Aquino and her five brothers and sisters, whose family name is Cojuangco, and is an exemplar of the plantation economy which is still at the heart of Filipino agriculture.

In a land where as much as half of the total workforce depend on the land for a living, and where the government's own figures show that seventy per cent of the population live below the poverty line, the issue of land reform and social justice is a key one. During her presidential election campaign Cory Aquino vowed that if elected she would implement land reform, starting with her own family's estate.

The Hacienda Luisita has more than 6,000 hectares (15,000 acres) of land of which 5,400 are given over to the cultivation of sugar cane, producing around 350,000 tons in an average year. Its owners like to think of it as a model estate which thanks to modern methods produces double the yield per hectare of its neighbours and offers better than average pay and conditions to its workers.

Of the land not given over to sugar some 120 hectares are used to house the hacienda's workers and their families, an estimated population of 24,822 men, women and children. Some 184 hectares are set aside for the residences of the six Cojuangco families and their swimming pools, outdoor jacuzzi, guesthouses, racecourse, stables for racehorse breeding, fishponds, and a private airstrip which was about to be refurbished at the time I visited. The estate includes a 200-hectare golf course, for which the grass seed was shipped from Hawaii. The private land also has hutches for the Cojuangco men's 1,000 gamecocks which they fight in their private 200-seater high-tech cockpit. Each bird has its own individual accommodation, which is more than can be said for the Cojuangcos' workers, many of whom sleep in dormitories of more than 200 people.

Another part of the estate had recently been turned into a 400-hectare industrial estate on

which four companies were preparing new factories. One was a Japanese company which was transferring its operations to Luisita from Taiwan because workers there had begun to command increasing wages. The labour costs were at that time five times cheaper in the Philippines.

The hacienda was bought by Cory Aquino's father in 1958 with a government loan which was given on condition that after ten years the land would be distributed to the farmers. It never happened, despite a couple of half-hearted attempts to enforce it by President Marcos who regarded the Cojuangcos as his political opponents.

But despite the election promises land reform was not made a priority by the Aquino government. It was only after a demonstration by peasant farmers, which ended with thirteen of them being shot dead on the Mendiola Bridge outside Mrs Aquino's presidential buildings, that she launched what she entitled the Comprehensive Agrarian Reform Programme, which became known by what turned out to be an apt acronym: CARP. The details she decided to leave to the national Congress. It was a recipe for disappointment. Most of the congressmen were themselves landowners and one of the most influential was Congressman José Cojuangco, Cory's younger brother who runs Hacienda Luisita and heads the Cojuangcos' financial empire.

The landlords peppered the land reform legislation with loopholes. One of them was that on an estate like Luisita instead of distributing

Seasonal workers like this man do not benefit from land reform proposals. They do not even get the £1 a month substitute-for-land allowed under the land reform. They eat and sleep in cramped cubicles in vast dormitory sheds. The wages are so low that at the end of the season many have saved nothing to take home.

the land to the workers, the owners could turn the land into a limited company and distribute stocks. By clever accounting the estate's business was then subdivided into seven corporations, only one of which involved the land. And even in that one most of the value was assessed in the machinery, irrigations systems, and value of the standing crops: as a result only 33.3 per cent of the value of the company was said to be the land and so the stocks the workers are to be given, over the next thirty years, will never represent a controlling interest. In the event the stocks will pay the workers a dividend of about forty-seven pesos a month (just under £1).

The president of the United Luisita Workers' Union says the sugar workers are happy with this. When I met him, with the hacienda chief administrator helpfully translating his remarks, he said: 'People voted for the stock option by a ninety-seven per cent majority because that was the best deal for us. If the land had been distributed we wouldn't have got enough each to live off and we don't have the management or marketing expertise to run it as a co-operative. This way we get stocks, we get bonuses on sales and profits and we get a 240 square metre plot given to us free to build a home on. There are no problems here between union and management because the owners are very kind people.'

One by one they appeared out of the darkness. The meeting was illegal and they had had to slip by the plantation's armed vigilante units. Those attending had come from most of the eleven *barrios*, as the villages are known, on the Hacienda Luisita. There were eighteen of them crowded on to the small benches placed on the mud floor of the hut in which one of them lived. They were the leaders of Ambalus, the rebel sugar workers' union formed by those who felt that the official union was too much in the pocket of the Cojuangco family.

Outside, Mabilog *barrio* was about its evening business. There was a steady trade in the tiny *sari-sari* stores, little wooden kiosks attached to the front of some of the houses made from corrugated iron and rough-sawn wood, which carried a little of everything for those who had not bought sufficient on their last visit to the town market. A hot-dog seller was grilling individual sausages to order on the small home-made barbecue which served as her stall. The little knots of men and women stood gossiping in the darkness on the dusty street corners.

Inside the hut only the Ambalus president was missing. Alex Gonzales, who had set up the meeting and arranged to smuggle us into the hacienda for it, had thought it prudent not to attend. He had been fired from his job driving a cane-cutting machine not long after Ambalus became active and sneaked back only occasionally for fear of repercussions on those the vigilantes heard he had visited.

The picture the Ambalus men painted was rather different from that outlined by the management and by the official union leader. The minimum wage was 108 pesos (£2.25) a day, they agreed, but often they worked only two days a week and even in the good times there were massive deductions from their pay. A number of them flourished payslips in evidence.

One forty-nine-year-old sugar worker who had grown up on the hacienda and worked there all his life, produced his. After deductions his take-home pay was 9.5 pesos (nineteen pence) for every day worked. 'That's the minimum living allowance. They're not allowed to deduct that. It will pay for half a kilo of rice and a little salt and sugar. The rest goes to pay off the loans.'

Few of them earned enough to be able to save. 'The money all goes on food. So when there's an emergency you have to borrow', said another

who had worked there since 1942. The sugar workers borrowed for all manner of things – to pay for medical treatment, for education, for clothes, even for food – there was a 'rice loan' which could be obtained during the slack season and repaid during the busy months. One man's 36,000 peso (£750) 'calamity loan' was needed to build a new house after the old one was destroyed by a typhoon. It would take him, his wife and his sons five years to pay it off and in that period they would be able to buy nothing else – the plastering, painting and construction of floors would have to wait.

On the issue of the whole land reform process the account given by the Ambalus men was also quite different from the official version of the hacienda management. They were in no doubt that the stock distribution scheme was little

There are one thousand fighting cocks on the hacienda. Each has its individual hutch, which is more than can be said for the estate's workers. The family also has riding stables, a racecourse, an airstrip and a golf course, for which the grass was shipped from Hawaii.

more than a fraud to deny them the genuine land reform Mrs Aquino once promised. 'We were promised land that we could farm and call our own. But when it comes down to it they are fobbing us off with forty-seven pesos a month. It is enough to buy about four kilos of rice,' said one.

'The workers were never offered a real choice between land distribution and the stock option. They gave us only four days' notice of the referendum. We complained that this was insufficient time to present our case but they said it could not be postponed. We set up a mobile patrol to present the facts in the different *barrios*. But we weren't allowed to go in to speak to people. We prepared leaflets and all these were stolen from us and destroyed,' another man said, in a burst of indignation.

'At the same time the overseers were going round telling everyone that if they didn't vote the right way they would be blacklisted and not given work,' said a third worker. 'The union leaders said that anyone who voted "No" would be expelled from the union and lose their job.'

At this point a bottle of Coca-Cola was produced from the back of the hut. It was carried with ceremony on an old tin tray with a small tumbler, opaque from much washing. It had been bought from the *sari-sari* store for the visitor. The eighteen poor sugar workers sat and watched with smiles as it was poured for me.

'When the referendum came it was a secret ballot. But the ballot papers were numbered and names were recorded against each number. It was clear that the management could find out how you had voted if they wanted to. Ambalus boycotted the vote but when the result was published it was clear that someone had voted on our behalf and they had voted "Yes",' explained one of the rebels.

'They also allowed all kinds of people to vote – overseers, outsiders, the children of super-visors, retired workers, even the names of people who were dead appeared on the list. They boosted the numbers from the real figure of 3,776 to over 6,000 to enable them to claim that if there was land distribution everyone would get only 0.7 hectares, which would not be sufficient to grow enough for a family to live off.'

'Anyway,' one of his fellows interjected, 'we would not turn the land over to food production. We would continue to grow sugar. The milling centre would still exist, and the Cojuangcos would still own it. They would still make a profit from the milling. But the land would belong to us.'

They went to the different agencies of the government to protest – but without success. Now, with the help of Sentra, a legal rights centre which is one of Christian Aid's partners in the Philippines, they were about to petition the Supreme Court. 'But we will wait until the cane-cutting and milling is complete and the slack season begins so that they can't subject us to further harassment by withdrawing work.'

Outside, Mabilog *barrio* was preparing for sleep. The lights were flickering off in the tiny *sari-sari* stores. The hot-dog seller was packing up her meagre supply of sausages and raking the ashes of her little fire. The little knots of gossip broke up and headed for bed.

Congressman José Cojuangco said he would be interviewed not at the hacienda but at his 'official residence' in Manila. He was not going to the country that weekend, said his aide, with an uncertain smile, as the Congress was breaking up and Don José would be spending the recess in Australia as he always did.

The official residence was a single-storey building in a guarded enclave whose quiet tree-lined streets made it seem miles from the hubbub and traffic of ordinary Manila life, though it was in fact set in the middle of the sprawling capital's conurbation.

José Cojuangco was a polite and dapper man with the hard and rumpled face of a street-fighter and the spotless white trousers of a man who these days sees the streets only through the windows of an air-conditioned limousine. He ignored the plush white sofas which filled the room and sat in a hard, high-backed wooden chair at a table. His conversation was punctuated by the screeches of the mynah birds which peered inquisitively from a number of cages outside the window.

'The objective of agrarian reform is to improve the lot of the people tilling the land. That doesn't necessarily mean land distribution. It would be very hard for them to run the land themselves. Where there was distribution in the late 1950s and 60s the land has, by now, ended up in the hands of a few owners.'

The first of a succession of ghostly servants appeared and silently laid dishes of sweetmeats on the table. The first of a succession of beautifully dressed daughters entered the room and, without speaking, kissed their father on the forehead, as they made their progress in and out of the house.

Stock distribution was the obvious answer in Luisita, he said. With a cold courtesy he responded to the complaints of his employees. The ballot had been truly secret, he maintained. 'Yes, we allowed everyone to vote. What were we supposed to do? Leave people out? It seems to me that those who oppose it are running out of things to complain about . . .

'May I point out something,' he said, leaning forward for the first time in the conversation. 'We've been accused of opting for this for our own purposes. In fact the best option for our family would have been to sell the land to the government under the CARP programme. Even at the lowest valuation that would be worth 250 million pesos (£5.2 million), which at ten per cent interest would be twenty-five million a year. There's only six of us that own it. That would mean we'd make four million plus a year, which is far more than we make now. Why don't we do this? Because of our social obligations.'

The air was rent with a shriek of outrage from one of the birds. Progress on land reform would be slower than some people might want, he said. Progress in most areas was slow.

Congressman José Cojuangco runs the hacienda Luisita and the Aquino family's financial empire. The family would make more money if they sold the estate to the government for distribution to peasants, he says. Instead they stick with the hacienda 'because of our social obligations.'

Tating Pedro has lived on an Imok plantation in the Philippines since he was a boy of seven. He harvested coconuts for the owner and planted his own subsistence crops between the trees. Now he has been thrown off the land so that it can be redesignated as 'industrial' to exempt it from land reform.

FACING PAGE: *All the peasants of Imok have been evicted from the land their families have farmed since 1919. The women continue to wash in the local river. But the men are forced to travel into the capital, Manila, to find work on building sites. They come home only at weekends.*

All the old man was doing was harvesting the beans he had planted the year before. Suddenly from behind a clump of banana trees the three armed guards appeared and menacingly waved their rifles at him. The old man was afraid. He knew that another farmer had been shot dead not far from there.

Tating Pedro had harvested in the same spot for fifty-six years since he was a boy of seven. He had worked all his life on the coconut plantation at Imok, a small village in Laguna, two hours to the south of Manila. When there was no work with the coconuts he and the other farmers worked on their own crops which they planted between the tall palms which towered sixty feet above.

It was just after dawn. Back in the village the other old men were drinking hot sweet coffee on the doorsteps of their ramshackle wooden huts. The women were sweeping the earth outside their kitchens with long-handled brushes which left broad curving patterns in the dust. The young men were standing by the road waiting for their Monday morning ride into Manila where they would work until the next weekend, as house painters or builders' labourers, now that there was no work on the land.

Pedro had said that, as it was Monday, the guards would not appear until well after dawn. He offered to show me around the place where he had worked all his life. On the way back he saw the beans and stopped to pick. But he became absorbed in his work, anxious to gather as much as he could for there would be no other food that week, and he lost track of time.

The three men bore down on him. They carried only ancient Brownings but they were dangerous enough for Pedro. Their leader began fiercely to shout questions at him. It is difficult to know what might have happened had I not intervened.

The plantation at Imok is owned by Desederio de los Reyes who is the brother of Ting-Ting

Cojuangco, the wife of the Congressman José Cojuangco, such is the nature of the tight oligarchy which owns and runs the country. It is a small plantation of 224 hectares planted with coconuts. For decades the produce had been shared between the landowner and the farmers; the coconuts were split seventy per cent to the landowner and thirty per cent to the farmers, and the other produce seventy-five per cent to the peasants and twenty-five per cent to the landowner.

But in 1985 the landowner decided he would apply to have the land reclassified as industrial land in order to make a large profit in a future sale. The peasants were forced off the land which the oldest of them have inhabited since 1919 and told they were not allowed to harvest what they had planted between the palms. They were served notice to quit their homes but, in fact, were not evicted. But they were told that they were not allowed to repair or maintain their houses or build new ones for their children. Tating Pedro had lived there since 1935. In 1989 a typhoon hit his house causing severe damage, so he patched it up. But after the repair the landowner sent in his men to demolish the house. Pedro was away at the time. His wife and sick children were thrown out and the house was burned to the ground.

But the peasants refused to leave. Some of the young men, when they married, began living with their families in the cramped spaces beneath the floors of their parents' homes. They enlisted the help of the local office of Sentra in a legal battle to establish their rights to the land under the land reform programme.

From time to time the people of Imok continued to enter the plantation to harvest. Their
actions have caused a series of clashes. In one
a peasant was shot dead by the landlord's men.
In another the local army garrison was brought
in to intimidate the farmers; its commanding
officer accused them of being supporters of the
Communist rebels. The last incident was three
months before I visited Imok when four guards
shot at peasants trying to harvest coconuts.

Most of the farmers became too frightened
to enter and Tating Pedro is now among their
number. 'There are many people against us,' he
said. 'In theory we are eligible to be granted
the land under the land reform programme.
We qualify. But I do not know if it will ever
be granted. The odds seem loaded against us.'

Success will not depend simply upon whether
they are right in law, said Sentra's regional co-
ordinator, Joanne Diozon. 'There was a similar
situation in Yulo. Land was reclassified as industrial to make it exempt from the CARP, even
though in practice it remained agricultural land.
But the peasants' association was well organized
there. As well as challenging the reclassification
in court, they put up resistance on the ground,
and won. More and more we are coming to see
that it is important for Sentra to get in before
there is a legal problem and do some work on
building up the peasants' organization to enable
it to resist.'

Those who win in court and on the ground
then find that they are faced with a new set

*The people of Imok have no land but the
landowner tolerates their living in their old
homes on the edge of the plantation. But no
new houses can be built. So families like that of
Sylvia Gutiérrez live in the tiny spaces between
the stilts of their parents' home. They crouch
perpetually.*

Even in their cramped homes the people of Imok find space to create small shrines. The hands came off the statue of San Antonio during a typhoon. 'He is now a handless saint for hopeless people,' said one peasant, sarcastically.

FACING PAGE: *A roadside banner announces that the people of Imok intend to resist attempts to expel them from their homes. They have enlisted the help of Sentra, a citizens' advice group funded by Christian Aid, in their legal battle to establish their rights to the land under the Philippine land reform programme.*

of problems. All too often those who gain land lose it after a few years. 'It is becoming clear that just getting the land is not enough', said Sentra's national legal officer, Marvic Leonen. 'The poor are starting from the bottom and so need a whole network of support services. They may need access to loans for capital equipment to get started. They need to have training in how to form and manage the co-operatives which will enable them to buy and sell in bulk at better prices. They need good local road networks to be built so that they can get their produce to market. They may need farm-to-market loans to tide them over until their produce is sold.

'Without all this it is not surprising if the poor do give up and sell the land to rich neighbours or lose it to the bank when their debts get out of control. Land reform can only work if

it is part of an overall package of measures to help the poor farmer.' Under Cory Aquino the opposite has been the case. Easy lending programmes for farmers have been dropped. Subsidies on fertilizer have been abolished. Agricultural agencies have been privatized or deregulated. 'The resources needed to make land reform work have just not been allocated. It is a sign of a real lack of seriousness.'

A thick red carpet ran over the dark mahogany floor which led to the study of Cardinal Jaime Sin, Archbishop of Manila, and fomenter of the pivotal action in the 1986 revolution against the dictator Ferdinand Marcos. In an air-conditioned room he worked in his full cardinal's robes. Such were the cushioned cloisters which

Sister Christine felt compelled to abandon.

His view of Mrs Aquino's period of office was less critical. 'Mrs Aquino took over with a very big problem. Marcos had been entrenched as a dictator for twenty years. He destroyed our democratic structure. He left the military strong and dictatorial. There was no way to bring your grievances to the courts because even these were under the influence of the dictator. The newspapers were controlled by him. Those who spoke out against him were liable to end up in prison or to just disappear.

'Mrs Aquino's great achievement has been the restoration of democracy and the democratic structures – restoring the independence of the executive, the legislature and the judiciary. She has written a constitution which was overwhelmingly ratified by the people. She has conducted national elections for the Senate and the Congress. She has conducted local elections for governors, mayors and *barrangays*. The Supreme Court is now respected by everyone and nobody influences it. All this has been a great achievement.'

But on the subject of land reform the cardinal-politician suddenly became uncharacteristically other-worldly: 'The Church can persuade the rich to give away their wealth; this can only be done gradually but the Church is working very hard on this now.'

The people had expected more on issues like land reform, I suggested. 'She was not prepared for that job.' said the cardinal. 'She was just chosen by the people because she was the only person who could defeat Marcos. The woman is a pure housewife. What more could you expect from a housewife? In the circumstances she has achieved a lot.'

Others disagree utterly. 'The whole thing is a con.' said Jaime Tadeo, the peasant farmers' national leader, when I visited him in his maximum security prison cell a few days later. He was jailed after a demonstration outside the Department of Agrarian Reform when farmers padlocked its doors on the grounds that it might as well be shut. 'After five years of Aquino promises the situation is worse than ever. In 1990 only twenty-two hectares of private land were distributed. A lot of the so-called distributions are just the formal handing over of titles to land which farmers already own. We had reservations when she came to power because she was from

People power on the streets made Cory Aquino President of the Philippines. She promised land reform and many other changes. But true reform has not come and Cory has continued to repay the massive foreign debts incurred by the Marcos regime.

The ribbons of the demonstrators flutter in the wind like the hopes of the landless peasants of the Philippines.

a landed family and she had never experienced poverty. But we hoped that she would do better because of what happened to her husband. But she has been a complete let-down.'

The square before the Central Post Office was full of women. They were there, in theory, to celebrate National Women's Day but the event had turned into a spontaneous protest against Mrs Aquino. 'Cory, you are a disgrace to Filipino women,' read one of the placards carried by tens of thousands of women gathered from all over the Philippines – women farmers, lawyers, workers, students, trade unionists, and women doctors.

They were sporting a new colour. The yellow of Mrs Aquino's People Power had gone and in its place was the violet of Gabriela, the women's organization. The violet garlands were everywhere – on flags, on sashes, on shirts and blouses, in headscarves and woven into the straw of hats to protect the women from the heat of the midday sun. Women from the towns near US military bases carried anti-prostitution banners festooned in violet. Even the nuns at the gathering had tied violet ribbons across their wimples or fastened them to the sleeve of their habits.

It was a scene reminiscent of those five years ago but this time the slogans were different. There was much indignation about the level of the Philippines foreign debt – but the anger was not now against Marcos for incurring their crippling national debt; it was against Cory for her agreement to honour even the most immoral of Marcos's dealings. There were protests about the 'Letter of Intent' Mrs Aquino had signed with the International Monetary Fund which the protestors said was designed to improve the country's balance of payments at the expense of the poorest sections of society. But noticeable among them were a number of placards which recorded a contemptuous verdict on the Aquino land reform programme.

They marched towards the presidential palace. But about a kilometre from its gates they were stopped by an assembly of armed troops who sheltered behind two lines of razor wire. Behind them were vehicles with water cannons at the ready.

The wire was stretched across the Mendiola Bridge which, in the mythology of Filipino protest, is the dividing line between the city and the government, between the people and the ruling elite. It was here in 1987 that thirteen peasant farmers were shot dead by government troops as they marched on the palace to demand that Mrs Aquino should honour her promises on land reform after a year of inactivity. In an attempt to erase that memory Mrs Aquino renamed the bridge after Don Joaquin Roces, one of the key participants in the 1986 revolution which brought her to power. The monument erected in his honour speaks of the bridge as 'the dividing line between the forces of oppression and the deprived people of this nation'.

The women marched right up to the monument and the wire. On the other side the armed men braced themselves. The protestors stood there for a few pregnant moments and chanted. Then they tied their violet ribbons to the hard edges of the wire where they fluttered, like the hopes of the landless peasants of the Philippines, on the wind.

5 | Taking Possession of the Land

Land reform through war in Eritrea

The meeting was due to start at two o'clock. But peasant farmers judge time by the sun and ignore even that if something more immediate demands their attention. Osman Idris was an hour late but he was one of the first to arrive. It was another two hours before enough of the others had trickled in for the meeting to begin. Eventually about sixty of them had gathered beneath the large tree where they sat in a semi-circle, their pickaxes placed in front of them like symbols of their office. At the back, a little away, their faces veiled in the display of public modesty considered appropriate to Muslim wives, sat five of the women who worked with the men.

The officials who were to address the gathering had been honoured with chairs from the village school. They sat uncomfortably on the junior-sized seats. A young woman official from the Eritrean government's agricultural department was there to give a report to the farmers. She wore trousers and no veil as if to show that things really were changing.

'Things are going well. Before, some people were giving priority to their own problems and ignoring the communal work but this is not happening now', she concluded, after outlining progress on the terracing, the reafforestation scheme and the building of canals and dams to conserve water. 'We have put in some hard work and if good rains come it will have a really noticeable effect on the harvest. Any questions or points?'

A farmer at the back asked: 'Why have the work gangs been made bigger? If we made more gangs, with fewer in each, they could get some work done on everyone's land before the rains. As it is some land will be done well and some not at all.'

The reply came from the floor of the meeting. It was Osman, as the leader of one of the gangs, who spoke: 'When we had smaller gangs and a couple of people were absent the gang was useless. This way is more effective. Don't worry. We will get around all the land. We will work harder.'

Some days later I met Osman out with his gang. They had started early, determined to finish all the work before the date when the rains were due. They were standing discussing a terrace of broken-down stones which sagged across a hillside near the school. It was in the wrong place. That was clear. Osman stood with a pickaxe in one hand and placed the other on his hip as he listened to Idris Ibraheem, the peasant farmer who owned the small plot of land.

Idris explained how, when the rain had come, the first terrace had worked. It had held back the soil and formed a good level area for planting the barley. But this second terrace had proved a failure. The torrential rain had washed along it and round the edge, carrying the life-giving soil away with it. It would have to be rebuilt – and in a different place. The two men discussed the lie of the land.

There were thirteen men – and one woman – in the work gang. Since the land reform each had their own land which they worked three

days a week. But for three other days they came together to work communally on terracing work designed to halt soil erosion and improve the yields of wheat and barley produced on the steep highland slopes. Osman set them to work. Half began to lever out the rocks from the old terrace using their one and only crowbar and their bare hands. The rest began to rebuild it two yards further up the slope.

As the double row of stones took shape Osman began slowly to alter the line of the terrace. Two hours later it curved like a smile across the face of the hillside. The faces of the workers reflected its shape as they surveyed it for a moment. Then they packed up and moved on to the next task.

Eritrea is one of the few countries in the world where a programme of land reform has been extensively implemented which has put

Coffee is expensive in Eritrea, even though it is grown not far to the south in Ethiopia. Once Asha Mohamed Said, like the other women and men of Rora Habab, could afford it only rarely – they were feudal tenants and too poor. Now thanks to a land reform programme they reap the full benefit of the land and drink coffee regularly.

land in the hands of the poorest sections of the community. The reform has occurred over more than a decade as the Eritrean People's Liberation Front (EPLF) gradually took over sections of what was until recently the northernmost province of Ethiopia. It was only in May 1991 that they took control of the entire province after finally defeating the forces of the Ethiopian government. It brought to an end a conflict which had begun as long ago as 1962 when the former Italian colony was forcibly absorbed into Ethiopia by the Emperor Haile Selassie.

The land reform has been a piecemeal process. Eritrea is a land of many different cultures – highland and lowland, settled and nomadic, arable and pastoral, Christian and Muslim. The degree of change has varied in each region, influenced by local tradition, by the modifications made by the various rulers of the province at different periods. But one of the few advantages of the war has been that it has enabled the victorious side, the EPLF, to brush aside any opposition to land reform from those rich enough to have a vested interest in obstructing it. For the EPLF, which has a broadly socialist approach, land reform has been a priority based on the principle that those who farm the land should also control it.

In Osman's home in Rora Habab in the northern mountains the social situation was, until reform only a decade ago, like something from medieval Europe with peasants tied to the land as serfs, forced to work their landlord's land for no wages, and compelled to pay him tribute

The monthly meeting to discuss ways of raising crop yields provokes lively and good-humoured discussion at Rora Habab in Eritrea. Once these farmers worked for feudal landlords. Owning their own land has generated a new self-esteem among them.

The villagers of Meshal on the high Eritrean plateau must pray outside their church. There is not enough water for them to bathe and they cannot enter the church unless they are ritually clean. At every service they pray for rain.

PREVIOUS PAGE: *The period of land reform in Eritrea has coincided with a decade of devastating droughts. Everywhere the land is parched. Will the reform have raised productivity? The peasants wait for a year of good rains to find out.*

from their own meagre produce at certain key points of the calendar.

It was a Friday, the Muslim holy day, so there could be no work. Friday was a day for meeting, for talking and for drinking coffee. Osman invited me to his home to drink the beverage which is expensive but which is regarded as a food rather than a luxury throughout Eritrea and Ethiopia. His neighbour, Saleh Ibrahim, would be coming. He was a good man to meet, Osman said, for he had once been to the house of the *kentebay*, as the feudal chieftain who ruled the area was known.

Osman's wife Asha roasted a tiny handful of green coffee-beans in a small blackened pan over the open fire in the middle of their windowless hut of wood and stone. The beans were ground with a small piece of root ginger in an ancient wooden pestle and brewed in a tiny pot, no more than five inches high. The ritual performed by the woman of the house was long and elaborate. The chipped and cracked coffee cups and the battered old enamel plate on which they stood were washed and rewashed. The coffee was brewed and rebrewed, with cold water poured down the narrow funnel every time it threatened to boil over.

During the long ceremony Saleh took command of the conversation and began to speak of the days of the *kentebay*. 'I was born here, as was my father before me. In my father's time the land was owned by Kentebay Osman, a strong chief who lived at Nacfa, further into the mountains. He used to send soldiers here to seize goats and cattle. The people lived in fear of him.

'My father farmed for him three *tsemdi* – a *tsemdi* is the area which one man can plough with two oxen in a single day. When my father died I was allowed to carry on farming two of them and my brother was allocated one by the representative. The representative was the *kentebay's* overseer; he lived here and he could take land from you and give it to someone else. He was a powerful man and he had to be appeased with gifts just as did the *kentebay*. If you went to Sudan you would have to bring back a length of cloth or some sugar for him, or if his son married you would have to give him a gift of money.

'When Kentebay Osman died his two sons divided the land between them. This part belonged to Kentebay Hassan. He used to send twenty camels each year to collect the harvest. He never came here but I met him once in Nacfa when I went there to take him two goats on the occasion of his son's wedding. Why did I give? Today I wonder. But then it was part of the natural order. I hoped for favour and that he would give us more land.'

Only once did the *kentebay* arrive in Rora in person. 'Kentebay Hassan lived in the town of Keren, many miles away. During the war the Ethiopians took the town and Kentebay Hassan fled here. He came on a horse with his servants and with many camels which carried all his belongings. He was received with great honour. The best bed in the village was taken to the best house. We made new mattresses for him. After he had settled we all went to pay court to him. He was a big man, fat and strong, with red shoes and a watch. His clothes were very clean and he had an expensive shawl. The representatives surrounded him. They tried to keep us away in case we persuaded him to give us land. But we were allowed to kiss his hand and take him gifts. I gave him two goats.'

'I gave him fifty Sudanese pounds,' said Osman. 'I hoped that he would give me land. But he gave me none.'

The feudal ruler departed for the safety of neighbouring Sudan. Every year the fruits of the harvest were sent to him until the EPLF consolidated its hold on the area and introduced land reform which redistributed the land to those who tilled it.

Has the reform been a success? In one way it clearly has. There is a personal dignity to Osman and his fellows which is enriched by the sense they have of controlling their own lives. It is a quality which does not belong to the state of serfdom. Men and women can only be truly free and fully human when they are able in some part to shape their own destiny. But there is another important aim of land reform, according to Stephanos Seyoum, the head of Eritrea's national Agricultural Commission. 'Our primary concern was with equity – we wanted to distribute the land to those who till it – but we also want to raise national productivity.' Unfortunately the period of land reform has coincided with a decade of devastating droughts across Sahelian Africa. 'We have had one or two good years when the rains have come. Then we have seen yields double and even quadruple in some areas. But most of the years we have had no rain. So it is hard to judge whether land reform has been completely successful.'

In the steep valleys next to Osman's the landscape had taken on the blasted appearance of an area devastated by a nuclear bomb. In many places not a drop of rain had fallen for two years. The soil there was a lifeless monochrome with not a single plant to enliven it and whole hillsides were covered in dead trees, their branches hanging broken from previous years when farmers snapped them to feed their leaves to livestock which is itself long dead. The day before I had come across Osman engaged in a similar activity in his own valley. Perched high in the branches of a *shamut* tree he was stripping the branches of every inch of foliage to throw it down for fodder for his goats. 'What else can we do? In previous years we left some leaves on every tree here to keep it alive. But this year there is so little grazing that we have to take everything. The tree may die next year, but that is better than all the animals dying this year.'

The traditional strategy for Eritrean men in this situation is to leave their families and go off to Sudan for six months in search of casual work. In an attempt to stop this and to build upon the foundation of the land reform the Eritrean Relief Association, the indigenous development agency, has initiated an integrated development project, supported by Christian Aid, in the area. The backbone of the scheme – which includes clinics, schools, water conservation and reafforestation projects – is the terracing work to halt erosion and increase crop yields.

'The project is a godsend,' said Osman. 'We have work to do all year. The quality of the land is improving year by year as a result. It is difficult to disentangle the different influences. None of it would have happened without the land reform. But without the project the land reform would have meant nothing. Now what we need is rain.'

Three systems of land holding have existed in Eritrea since ancient times. Two of them, known as *tselmi* and *resti*, were forms of private ownership by which land could be passed from father to son, with a variety of special conditions and restrictions. Such were the systems which led to the building of the large *kentebay* land holdings. The other system, *diesa*, was a form of communal ownership by which land was held in the name of the village. What made it unique was that every seven years, or at a period dictated by local custom, the land was reapportioned to the village's families by lottery.

In Meshal village on the highland plateau between the Eritrean capital Asmara and the Ethiopian province of Tigre, the *diesa* system has been in operation for as long as collective memory can recall. In places like that the extent of the EPLF reform has been only to extend the categories of those eligible for land to include women and the *makailet-ialet*, landless migrant labourers like Giday Gebre Selassie. 'I have lived in this village for twenty years but I have never been eligible for land because I was not born here. I came from the city, from Mekele, many years ago and settled here. For years I just worked doing odd jobs – repairing houses, helping with ploughing or the harvest, shepherding which is considered a job for a child. In those days I think people had a regard for me but I was always an outsider. Now at the age of sixty-five I am at last an equal. It is only when you have your own land that you are a proper man.'

The requirements of social justice have a cost however. The inclusion of the *makailet-ialet*, along with the steady rise in population,

causes problems in a place like Meshal, as was explained by Kashi Tesfa Abraham, one of the committee of three elected by the villagers to supervise the sabbatical redistribution. 'The problem is that there is no place to expand. There is no more land. As people grow, each family's land gets smaller. How will this problem be solved? By God. Perhaps the hunger and the dying children are his solution.'

Stephanos Seyoum clearly has a less fatalistic view of God and sees the need for changes in systems of land holding. 'None of the traditional systems offers an ideal blueprint. The problems of *resti* are obvious enough in areas where a few people own a lot of land and the majority are landless and hungry. But the *diesa* system has drawbacks. It creates a disincentive to investment. When the land is to be revolved every

In Meshal, for as long as anyone can remember, the land has been redivided every seven years to those born in the village. But after land reform others, like Gidav Gebre Selassie, are included. 'I came here looking for work 20 years ago. Ever since I have been an outsider; but now I have land I am a proper man,' he said.

seven years people stop investing in it after the
fourth year, they stop terracing and manuring. It
means that there is no incentive to do long-term
work like digging canals, planting perennials
like coffee or citrus trees, or digging wells.

'So do we go for a one-off redistribution? That
may be fair now. But in fifteen years' time will
that system have become unfair? The problem
of population growth will become a chronic
problem in a country where industry is so weak
it cannot absorb the surplus population which is
unable to make a living on the land.'

One suggested solution is to encourage young
farmers from the highlands to go to the western
or eastern lowlands. 'But it would have to be
done by encouragement not coercion. We would
need capital to create the services to encourage
them, such as a health programme to deal with
the malaria they will find in the lowland areas.
But something will have to be done, especially
as the large number of Eritreans trickle back
from Sudan where they have been refugees from
the war.'

Many of the areas in the lowlands are currently
occupied by nomads practising a technique of
extracting the thinly-scattered resources of the
semi-desert margins which is so ancient that
it is often neglected in considerations of land
use. The past decade of drought has been so
severe that even these have undergone a major
setback. In the province of Barka I encountered
in the desert wastes two nomad families who had

*Every year the population grows. So
every Sabbath year, when the time for
redistribution arrives, the land is divided
into smaller portions. Soon the plots will
be too small to sustain a family. Will
there be enough land for this boy, seen
here cutting cactus to feed the family's ox,
when he grows up?*

hung the skins of fifty-three goats and sheep to dry from the branches of dead thorn trees. They were sadly representative. They had four animals left alive from a herd which had numbered more than 200 before the first of the severe droughts in 1984.

One of them, Adam Abdulla, said: 'That first drought had halved our flocks but this time things are far worse. Soon we will have no animals left at all.' The family had already given up moving along its traditional migration pattern and was squatting on the edge of the town of Germaica hoping for casual labour.

Another Eritrean Relief Association programme, also funded by Christian Aid, is designed to try to help. 'We have limited schemes to restock the herds of those who are worst hit. But we also have programmes of animal health care, with vaccination and the training of paravets, to try to encourage the nomads not to think of their wealth in terms of the sheer number of their animals; we want them to understand that quality not quantity is what counts, otherwise there will be terrible overgrazing,' said Stephanos Seyoum.

'In the end nomadism is a way of survival not development. Their contribution to the national economy is minimal. Of course we encourage them to settle and farm. And we're trying to get their children into school to educate them into other ways. Many don't want to but then everybody's happy in what he's doing until he's shown an alternative. They would like refrigerators and air conditioning if they were offered it.' Clearly the old Victorian theory that pastoralism is a stage of human development which is somehow more primitive than settled farming is not dead. Despite the fact that nomads actually squeeze resources out of marginal areas which could not otherwise be tapped, most African governments remain hostile to these uncontrolled and untaxed groups which

make no obvious contribution to the statistics on gross domestic product. The nomads, like the indigenous tribal peoples on other continents, are evidently those whose access to land seems most perilously vulnerable.

'We have to find the right blend,' said Stephanos Seyoum, who has instructed the Agricultural Commission to carry out a large-scale survey of all the different systems of land-holding in Eritrea. 'We are looking for a formula which is fair, which fits in with local tradition and which raises productivity. Of course there will always be a conflict between these three criteria and we have to find a way to strike the right balance.

'It may well be that different things are required in different parts of the country. Highland areas may need to be pump-primed with basic inputs like tools and oxen to restart production; there we need the money for training farmers in new techniques, to repair roads and build distribution mechanisms so that when farmers have grown extra produce it can be marketed. Lowland areas like Sheib may need high levels of capital investment for construction work and tractors and machinery.'

The hot season was upon the great plain of Sheib and the time was near when the people would move to the mountains until the winter. A few families had already dismantled their houses of bent poles and woven mats and packed them onto the backs of their camels and begun the week-long trip. Some had left early that morning and others the night before so that good headway could be made in the coolest times of travel.

It was the middle of the four hottest hours of the day, from just before midday until four o'clock in the afternoon, and the temperature in the shade of the hut of loosely-woven reeds was 105° Fahrenheit. The heat seemed to drain the strength from my muscles and make my limbs feel weak.

A group of men and women lounged around on rope beds or sat on straw mats on the floor. A goat had been killed in honour of the English visitor and we had all enjoyed a good lunch of fresh meat and maize porridge. Now they passed around a wide enamelled tray covered with enormous slices of watermelon which one of the men had fetched from the fields in the floodplain where one deluge provides enough water in a single miraculous burst to sustain the long slow growth of the giant fruit. It had been cut open for an hour and the slices exposed to the air; remarkably the evaporation of the juices cooled the fruit as effectively as would

OVERLEAF: *In many areas nomads now feel under threat as farmers slowly encroach on their best pasture land. The fear is that the farmers will devastate the marginal land by expecting too much from it. The process will drive nomads into inhospitable regions where their ancient traditions may quietly perish.*

A girl knocks seeds from a thorn tree for her goats to eat. On the margins of Eritrean society live an uncounted number of such nomads. For centuries they have used their animals as mobile stores to gather up the grass and rain which falls sparsely over a wide area. On the desert fringes it is often the only way of using land efficiently.

a refrigerator. One of the women sat constantly flicking a fan of grass to keep the flies off the glistening fruit. From a pole hung a goat-skin full of water, wet from the slow seepage through the pores which kept its contents as cool as any parched desert throat could crave. It was a system which the forebears of the men and women of Sheib had discovered many centuries before.

The talk was of their ancestors too and of the great lowland plain in former times. For centuries the area had been inhabited only by nomads, whose legacy was in evidence from the style of tented houses which the people there still occupied. Then, perhaps a century ago they thought, a group of aristocratic farmers from the highlands moved down to the dusty flatlands and began to establish farms. They brought with them serfs from their upland estates and, as they gradually laid claim to all the grazing areas of the nomads, gradually forced the nomads into dependency as day labourers.

Within a few generations the twenty main aristocratic families had 10,000 serfs in their thrall. For decades they practised the same crude form of flood irrigation, planting maize and sorghum in the land over which the floodwaters passed as they surged down from the mountains. 'It was a hard life. They paid us just enough to keep body and soul together. We had barely enough to feed our children. Life was just one long worry,' said one of the older men, prying fibres of meat from between his brown old teeth with the elongated nail of his little finger.

A farmer fetches water from his hut on the great plain of Sheib, in lowland Eritrea. Once 20 feudal overlords held 20,000 serfs in thrall here. Eleven years ago, when the area changed hands during a war, the land was handed over to the peasants. Crop yields have risen ten-fold.

The man sitting next to me was an amiable character in his early fifties. Black curls forced their way from under the pill-box hat ornamented with green and orange triangles which sat on the middle of his head. He had laughed and joked throughout the meal but suddenly he turned seriously to me and said: 'It was always my dream, while I was working for other people, that one day I would work on my own land. But I felt it was an impossible dream.'

Mohamud Mohammed Ali had no reason to think that his dream would ever come true. The system of land tenure had remained largely unaltered throughout this century. The Italians who colonized Eritrea left the system in place because the landlords were an easy way of maintaining control over the population and collecting a land tax from them. The British, who took over responsibility during the Second World War, abolished the feudal system of tributes but left the basic land relationships unchanged, as did the Ethiopian imperial regime of Haile Selassie which forcibly absorbed the region into Ethiopia in 1962. It was only in 1980, after the area came under the control of the Eritrean People's Liberation Front (EPLF), which was eventually to oust the Ethiopians entirely from Eritrea, that the feudal order was finally abolished.

'We had heard that the EPLF had instigated land reform elsewhere and we wanted it here too,' said Mohamud, who had previously been a labourer getting casual work from different landlords when he could find it, or journeying to the salt plains near Massawa when he could not.

'When the EPLF took this area we asked for land reform. They were cautious and studied the position for two years before acting. Then one day in 1980 they called a meeting to discuss the issue. More than 8,000 people turned up. The clear majority was for redistribution but there was heated discussion. Many of the landlords were there, and peasants who owed them favours. They began to quote the Koran. They said that taking your brother's land was a sin and that they would pray that God would punish us when we died. They said that if we took the land it would create bad blood which would endure for generations.

'A week later there was another meeting. This time the majority for redistribution was even greater. Again the landlords invoked the Koran but we replied that The Book said that God had created everyone equal, that land was created for all and that it was only buying and selling and snatching which had created the gaps which existed. We voted for reform and a week later it began.'

A committee of three was elected: a registrar, to list all those who laid claim to land; a measurer, who divided the land into parcels; and an eliminator, who struck people from the list if they were found to have land elsewhere or if they intended to be absentee farmers renting the land out to others. Every family was each given four *tsemdi*.

'For me the land reform has brought about a complete transformation. Before I was always worried whether I would survive from one year to the next. We ate just one meal a day. It was a very horrible hand-to-mouth life. Now life has become secure. I have a reasonable income and I can begin to accumulate wealth. So far I have two oxen, two cows, a donkey and two goats. My wife and children have new clothes. They eat porridge now with butter, sometimes even we eat meat. In the old days my wife would fetch water on her back for two hours each day and then wash clothes without soap. Now she has a donkey to carry the water and she uses Omo for the clothes – it is a detergent,' Mohamud explained proudly.

'It is as if I have had two lives in one lifespan. I have seen the world twice. But my pleasure is not

just in the improvement in my own lifestyle. I also see the life improving of people who were even more miserable than me. Under the new system there is help for the widow and for the man with no oxen. In the old days these people were reduced to begging. Now we have a committee which offers help from the community to these people. Nothing pleases you more than being able to help the orphan and the disabled. That's my pleasure.'

One of those beneficiaries was Fatna Cheway, a woman of fifty who has been a widow for the past twelve years. She sat on a mat in the corner of the room, shrouded in a robe of bright turquoise which she continually pulled over her head and up around her mouth so that only her eyes were visible. Occasionally there was a flash of the gold brooch which was set into the upper

There are two reasons for the striking rise in productivity at Sheib. Farmers level and plough with more dedication than serfs ever could. And the water-retaining dams on the great flood plain have been scientifically redesigned by the Eritrean Relief Association, supported by Christian Aid.

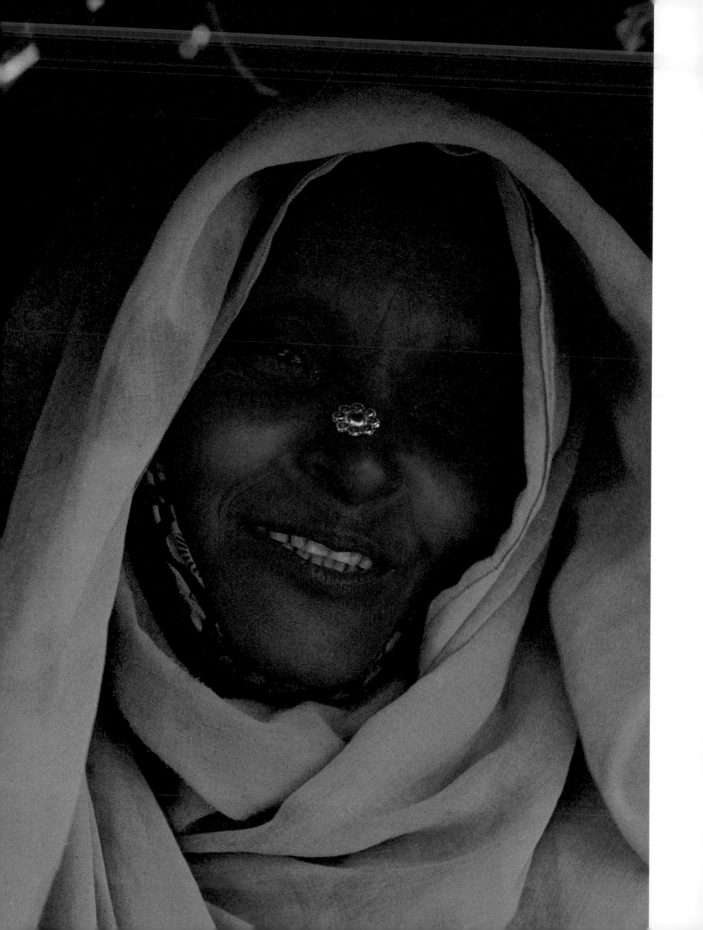

part of her nose. She spoke with the affectation of shyness adopted by Muslim women in that society. But land reform had changed one thing in that status. In previous times it was not possible in most parts of Eritrea for a woman to own land in her own right. Now Fatna owned four *tsemdi*, like everyone else.

'My father had two *tsemdi* of land but when he died I could not inherit. My husband was a poor man so when he died I had nothing, no income. I was forced to become dependent upon my brother. I had no change of clothing, my children were hungry for we had only one meal a day. I was living by God's grace.

'But now I have land and everything has changed. I cannot plough it myself but others plough it for me, for which I am doubly grateful. A woman cannot plough but I make food and tea for the men who plough for me and the others like me who cannot plough. Now I have an income, I can drink coffee and the children have sandals. Now we have three meals a day and sometimes we have yoghurt or butter in our porridge. Now I own a cow and a donkey.

'I am not an educated woman. I have no words to express my feelings. But if you could see into my heart you would know how deep is my thankfulness for the land reform.'

The sense of community engendered by the land reform has had dramatic effects on levels of productivity in Sheib. 'The traditional method of agriculture was just to use whatever water came

Under the land reform women were, for the first time, allowed to own land in their own right. The children of Fatna Cheway were once hungry but now, she says, 'we have three meals a day and sometimes we have yoghurt or butter in our porridge. If you could see into my heart you would know how deep is my thankfulness for the land reform.'

and try to divert it onto your land using sand dams which needed constantly to be rebuilt. Every person was concerned about his plot and didn't think about the rest. Since the land reform all that has changed. We now have an agricultural committee which has systematized the process of canals and dams so that the water is diverted in such a way as to obtain maximum use of it. The system retains almost every drop that comes down from the mountains. Very little is wasted,' said Mohamud who is now the deputy chairman of the committee.

Much of the work was masterminded by the Eritrean Relief Association. One of its agricultural officers, Tsegaye Yssac, who now lives with the people of Sheib, explained their strategy. 'We were able to bring in bulldozers and graders to build new stronger designs of dam which worked with the flow of the water rather than against it so that they didn't have to be repaired so often, which previously wasted a lot of working hours. The new system slows down the flow and ensures that every drop can be put to use. We took from among the farmers a few key people and taught them a completely new approach to agricultural construction, new ploughing methods, and educated them in the benefits of animal vaccination.

'All this is just the beginning. We have plans, which can be implemented now that a time of peace has arrived, to divert the entire course of the Maylala River and build a reservoir for all the fields of the plain which could then become a bread basket for the region. We would need foreign investment; we estimate it would cost $20 million, but we have shown that we can handle the technology. Productivity is up by 400 per cent.'

The striking rise in productivity has reconciled even some of the former landlords to the land reform. 'It is true,' laughed Hajji Mahamoud Gauder, who sat on one of the mats with his

legs folded with a suppleness which belied his seventy years.

'I was a landlord. When land reform was first suggested I couldn't accept it. Like most of the landlords I said that it was a sin to take your brother's land. There was a lot of resentment and many of the landlords left and went to Sudan. But I am glad I stayed. Now I see the benefits of working together. I used to have forty-five *tsemdi* which produced twenty quintals. Today with the co-operative system I get twenty quintals from just four *tsemdi*. Today when my brother starves, I starve; but when my brother prospers, I prosper too. Today I work harder; before I had four serfs and I worked with them on the land for six hours a day, now I work eight. But there is no sense of conflict in the community and I am happy.'

In Eritrea a family's wealth is measured by the number of animals it owns. Today the people of Sheib own record numbers. Many notches have now been worn in the side of the local well by the ropes which draw the water for the new livestock.

6 | The Drift to the Cities

Poor farmers flee the countryside

Nobody lives on the stretch of scrubby land between the flats and the petrol station at Jardim da Saúde any more. It seems strange to record the fact. Only a few weeks ago when I visited the place there were more than a hundred families living there in homes made of old doors, bits of wood and polythene sheets. Now, the news is, the site is empty.

So where are they now, that band of homeless people who had found a few months of refuge from the hostile anonymity of the streets of São Paulo in a small collection of haphazard shelters which they transformed into a community?

What of Maria Fraciosa da Costa? The twenty-two-year-old mother, with a baby on one arm and a toddler clinging to the other, had invited me into the home she and her husband had built from bits of wood begged from the other residents when they arrived eight weeks earlier. They had arrived in Jardim da Saúde after being asked to leave the lodgings of her sister – a single room, three metres square, in which they had lived for four months with four other adults and six children until her sister could bear the overcrowding no more. She was proud of the new place, even though its floor was of bare earth from which a penetrating damp rose, even though its furnishings consisted only of one bed and a home-made cupboard. The family's clothes hung like washing from lines of twine strung across the room. All their other possessions hung in plastic carrier bags from nails hammered into the uprights of the little shack. 'I was happy as it went up,' she told me.

'It was taking a risk, I knew. But my husband works in a soap factory and the wages there are not enough to cover the rent of a place, let alone buy any food afterwards. I was happy to have somewhere at last which was our own.' Where is Maria Fraciosa now?

What of Diogenes Cacio Castelo Branco? The effervescent young man was one of the committee of seven elected to lead the community. He had made contact with the city's main pressure group for the homeless, the Popular Housing Movement, and had participated in negotiations with the local authorities in their attempt to claim squatters' rights to the plot which the families had spontaneously occupied over a period of several months. He circulated around the settlement with an apt response for every circumstance – dispensing practical help to those who needed it, resolution to the waverers, kind words to those who looked distracted, and outrageous bonhomie to everyone else. In between it all he tried to teach me the syncopated rhythms of Brazilian folk guitar. If the police ever came, he said, he would resist. Where is Branco now?

And what of Maria Lucia Gomes Silva? She had once trained as an accountancy clerk but had been unable to find a job and had slipped from one catastrophe to another to end in one of the Jardim shacks. Life had once treated her better. That was evident from the array of belongings which surrounded her in the little hut she and her husband had made from sheets of bright purple hardboard. Compared with many

others in the camp she owned a lot – a gas stove, a sideboard, a wardrobe, two beds taken to pieces, an ironing board, two alarm clocks, a few books, piles of blankets and towels, a stack of cooking pans in a big cardboard box, a broom, a lampshade shaped like a doll and even a little pot of herbs. But the clutter of so many possessions in the cramped space seemed only to emphasize the indignity of this uncomfortable distillation of her life. Afraid of robbers, rapists and police, she sat awake all night in bed with a gun beneath the blankets while her husband was out on his job as a night driver. Where is Maria Lucia now?

A few weeks after my visit a large squad of riot police came and evicted them all. The land on which they were living belonged to the state authorities – ironically it was under the control of the body responsible for building houses for state employees but which cannot build for lack of cash. The squatters had tried to negotiate permission to stay there and even to get the city authorities to build a housing development for them. But the negotiations had failed and a court order had been issued to remove them. They had been turned onto the streets.

The occupation of land by homeless people at Jardim da Saúde was only one of dozens of such actions going on at any one time in Brazil's largest city. But the forces which drive people to the desperate act of land occupation, and which drove them from their rural homes in the first place, are not peculiar to São Paulo. All over the Third World millions of people who were once peasant farmers are abandoning the countryside, having been driven from the land by rich commercial farmers, by drought, by the

PREVIOUS PAGE: *Nobody lives on this stretch of scrubby land in the Jardim da Saúde any more. One morning, a large squad of riot police arrived and evicted 100 families.*

widescale flooding for hydroelectric schemes, by lack of work and by population explosions. But when they get to the cities – which from the viewpoint of rural penury often look like havens of golden opportunity – they find that life is little better and often a good deal worse. Landless farmers then become the urban landless creating a new set of problems which, trends indicate, will set a new and potentially explosive agenda for the Third World in the next century.

In 1800 only five per cent of the world's population lived in towns and cities. Today the overall figure is forty per cent. By 2010 more people will live in towns than live in the countryside. But these figures are worldwide. In the Third World the situation is more dramatic. The world's real urban revolution is taking place in the countries which have the health, sewage, education and transport infrastructures least able to cope with it.

Between 1950 and 1985 the urban population less than doubled in industrialized nations; in the Third World it quadrupled. Today in the West urban growth rates are slowing down and in some places cities are actually shrinking; in the developing world cities like Mexico and São Paulo are doubling in population in periods of less than twenty years. Within a decade three out of every four Latin Americans will live in towns or cities. London, which was in 1985 the world's ninth largest city, will be only the 21st by the year 1999. By the turn of the century nineteen of the largest cities on the planet will be in the Third World.

Brazil is a good example of the phenomenon of urbanization. In 1965 half the population lived in rural areas. Since then twenty million farmers have drifted into the cities. Today only twenty-five per cent of the population live in the countryside and by the year 2000 the figure will be down to a mere ten per cent. The consequences of this are far-reaching. Imagine,

for example, the amount of charcoal such urban populations require for heating and cooking and what the impact of that will be on levels of deforestation, which are already alarming. Imagine the amount of household rubbish produced in a city of nearly seventeen million people like São Paulo where most areas do not have refuse collection and people just throw their garbage into the nearest river or dump it by the roadside.

The causes of this drift to the cities are complex. The pattern will not be substantially reversed without changes in economic strategy and social policy in a number of areas by the national leaders of Third World countries and, just as significantly, by Western governments and the international agencies they control. Dealing with these would be beyond the scope of this book. But one element in the situation

Where are they now? This family had made their home in a hut of black plastic sheets and scrap wood. In the world's fastest growing city, São Paulo, they had been unable to find accommodation. So they joined a squat on land earmarked for public housing. It had been empty for years. But they were evicted.

At night this portrait of a Brazilian sea-goddess rested in the damp interior of a sticks and plastic hovel in the Jardim da Saúde squat. But this morning it was hung in the sun to give it air while the mistress of the hut swept up with an old broom.

is clear. Poor people will continue to flee the countryside until land reform is undertaken in a more comprehensive way.

Talk to almost anyone in the *favelas* of Brazil, or in the shantytowns outside Nairobi, or in the slums of Manila and the evidence is compelling. In Brazil I spoke to people in the slums of Rio de Janeiro and São Paulo, on the cocoa plantations in Bahia, in the prairie and dairy country of Paraná in the southern states. All told the same story.

Olimpio da Silva Matos, the president of the Popular Housing Movement in the southern zone of São Paulo, had come from Minas Gerais to the north of Rio where his grandfather had had 2,000 hectares of land. 'After he died we couldn't find the official titles to it. A local bigwig claimed it was his and the local judge, who was a friend of his, ruled that he could have it to put his cattle on. We were left with only a little land. As my grandfather and father both had twelve children there was not enough to go round. All you needed was for one harvest to fail and you'd fall behind with your debts so much you'd have to sell. So I came to the big city. What else could I do?'

Maria Fraciosa da Costa and her husband Jhodema from Jardim da Saúde had arrived in São Paulo after an odyssey around Brazil in search of the means to sustain a living. They had begun working on her father's land in the countryside of Piaui state but after successive droughts and poor harvests the young couple had left Maria's parents and their eight other children and moved to Teresina, the state capital, where Jhodema worked as a paid labourer. The work ran out after a year so they moved to the neighbouring state of Pernambuco where the work lasted for only two more years. So they decided to try their luck in São Paulo.

Dona Maria Silvia Matia left Minas Gerais when she was seventeen because her family lost their land when her father died after he was bitten by a snake. For the past forty years she has lived on the streets in São Paulo, often sleeping under a viaduct, collecting waste paper and sorting it to sell to recycling units. 'The work is hard. I get tired now that I am sixty. But I have made myself a trade by coming to the city.'

João André, from Maue, one of the biggest of the *favelas* in São Paulo, came from the state of Paraíba in the north-east which was once the heartland of Brazil's plantation prosperity. 'My family were always poor. We lived on other people's land, working it for them and getting a share of the harvest. Drought forced us to leave and look for work elsewhere. We travelled for eight days to Paraná in the south. We found work, again share-cropping, producing coffee.

But the land, which previously had been forest, became exhausted and yields fell. So it was cleared to make way for cattle. We tried to look for casual work but mechanized farming was being introduced in the area, producing soya beans to make animal food for export to Europe. Tractors meant fewer jobs for labourers and no land for subsistence farming so we came to the city. We arrived, but I could only find a very low paid job. We couldn't afford a house so I went to a *favela* and built a shack.'

People like these pour into the cities of the Third World every day. More than 200 families appear in São Paulo daily looking for a job, for accommodation and for schools for their children. Most of them have no money, little education and few marketable skills. Those who do find jobs try to find rented rooms in a *cortico*, the old tall tenement houses which have been subdivided into incredibly small rooms with incredibly high rents. The rest try to find an unused corner in one of the teeming *favelas*. Many, especially the children and teenagers, cannot find even that and live on the streets where, with no jobs available, prostitution and crime become norms. For a large number it ends in violent death; there are estimated to be 700,000 street children in Rio de Janeiro alone and every month some thirty or forty of them are killed by death squads of policemen or vigilantes intent on 'cleaning up' the streets.

The drift to the cities is, therefore, significant in two respects. Its sheer scale reveals just how desperate are those farmers without land in the countryside. But it also creates a new dimension to the issue of landlessness – as well as those without the land to grow what they need to eat, there are now rapidly increasing numbers of people without the land on which to erect even the most primitive of shelters.

There were homemade notices painted on scraps of wood fastened to fences and to the sides of the little wooden houses all along the alleyways of Casa Verde. '*Pedicure and manicure available here*,' said one. '*Frozen fruit juice for sale*,' read the next. '*Silk ties made here*,' announced the most improbable.

The signs advertised something more than the individual services or products on offer. They were evidence of a spirit of confidence and initiative among the people of a community which, two years before, had been as vulnerable and makeshift as the one in Jardim da Saúde which the police had broken up and dispersed.

Casa Verde is one of the examples of success for the Popular Housing Movement in São Paulo. It was first conceived by a group of people living in a poor area nearby called Vila Penteado. 'We used to meet in the priest's house after mass to discuss social issues and work out ways of improving our situation. That was four years ago. For a year we met and talked in general terms. Then someone came up with the idea of seizing a piece of land which belonged to one of the housing authorities but was standing idle. It was a desperate strategy but we knew we had to do something because most of us were living in rented places where the rent was rising much faster than our wages and we knew we would get thrown out eventually', said Ivone Tenorio Seabra, who has nine children and was one of the prime movers of the original Penteado group.

'We looked around for a suitable site and

Twelve million people live in São Paulo. Of them, some four million live in cortiços *– grand old houses which have been divided and sub-divided into the tiniest rooms imaginable. They range from the basic to the squalid and the rents charged by landlords can be exorbitant. Two men sleep in this room.*

found this place. It was owned by the CEF – the *Caixa Economica Federal*. It is a national insurance scheme whose funds are supposed to be used to finance housing for the poor. But in fact the only houses it has ever built have gone to the rich. So we began to plan to invade the land and occupy it.'

The land stood in a residential area of the city surrounded by tree-lined avenues of comfortable middle-class housing and high-rise flats. The first response of the authorities was to try to evict the 230 families from Penteado. But before they could act hundreds of other families had appeared – many of them from an overcrowded slum not far away known as Seaside Favela, perhaps in ironic reference to its location next to an open sewer. At one point there were 1,500 families on the site. The authorities abandoned the eviction plan and began to negotiate with the Casa Verde leaders.

'It was our first success but we knew we had a long way to go,' said the community's president, Paulina Maria da Conceicão da Silva, a thirty-six-year-old grandmother.

'The authorities' technique is to drag their feet to such an extent that the people give up,' warned Olimpio da Silva Matos, who had conducted similar negotiations in other parts of the city. 'I have had 122 meetings with the authority over one single site in the past two years. You have to keep at them. And you have to back up your negotiating with action – with demonstrations, with occupations. If you don't make life uncomfortable for them you'll never

A few of the homeless are fortunate enough to find derelict houses to sleep in. This one is the home of Dona Maria Silvia Matia who scrapes a living by collecting waste paper and sorting it to sell to recycling units. It has no roof so she sleeps under the floorboards.

get anywhere, however much in the right you may be morally or legally.' He was speaking at a meeting called by ANSUR, a co-ordinating body which works to create links between popular housing organizations in the different areas. ANSUR is funded by Christian Aid to help groups of the urban landless support one another. Through it they exchange information and experiences, and activists from the various land occupation groups receiving legal training.

Paulina laughed. 'They won't get rid of us that easily,' she said. The Casa Verde community had already embarked on a programme of direct action. They had conducted a number of demonstrations. They had hired buses to take them miles into the interior to the capital Brasília to lobby the housing minister. They had organized demonstrations which involved camping outside the CEF offices.

Their tenacity has secured a number of victories. The CEF has agreed in principle to hand the land over to the city housing authority so that proper houses can be built for almost all the occupants of the land. 'We are just arguing about valuations now.' They have secured piped water supplies to most parts of the community and the building of septic tanks for sewage disposal.

Inside Casa Verde the community has reordered the houses to create internal roads, improvised some drainage systems and created an electricity network. 'It's illegal at the moment. We are just tapping into the local system and taking it without paying for it. We have approached the electricity company and asked them to instal a proper system with meters. We must be one of the few groups who actually want to pay for something they get free at present.' She laughed again.

It was 8pm and the evening light was beginning to fade when the occupiers arrived at Vila Mariana in the south-eastern sector of São Paulo. They arrived in lorries and cars all at once and swiftly produced from the vehicles an impressive array of timber, roofing sheeting, tools, mattresses, a cooking stove and a motley collection of children.

The occupiers moved quickly into the teams which they had organized before arriving. One man began measuring the ground while the rest of his group began digging holes. A second group unloaded a selection of large timber beams and began to position them with wedges in the holes. A third team set to work with cross-beams and, within minutes, the roofing team had begun hammering the sheets to the beams. Beneath all this the gas light team was unpacking and lighting their lamps and hanging them from the new rafters. Around them the mattress team was preparing the bedding and inserting the children into it. The cooking team had set up the stove, lit it and got the supper under way. Smiles began gradually to fix themselves to the faces of the supervising team.

It was not long before the police arrived. When they did they were confronted by a human chain of men and women who sang as they stood with their arms linked. They were not the homeless and landless but supporters from local churches; the pastoral commissions of the diocese of São Paulo have been, under the direction of Cardinal Paulo Evaristo Arns, some of the most doughty supporters of the campaigns for homes for the poor.

Until that point the singers had been rendering

Many just sleep on the streets. But they do not give up hope or lose their dignity, as is clear from this neat cardboard home beneath a motorway flyover in the heart of São Paulo.

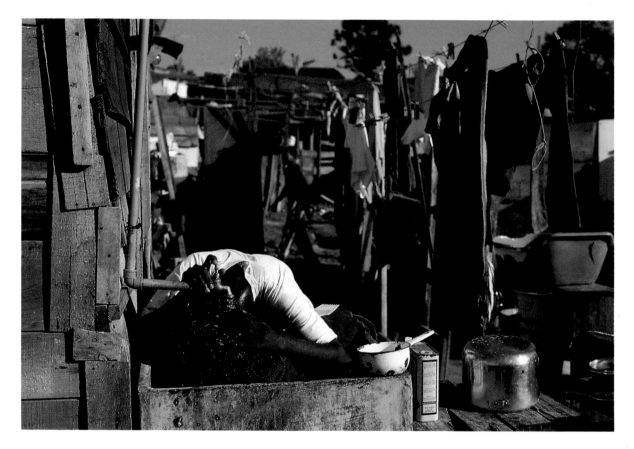

Facilities are still basic in Casa Verde but among the people there is a spirit of confidence and initiative. Homemade notices in the community's little streets announce the enterprise of the people. 'Pedicure and manicure available here,' says one. 'Frozen fruit juice for sale,' reads the next. 'Silk ties made here,' announces the most improbable.

PREVIOUS PAGE: *Some squats can be successful. Casa Verde was a great victory for the Popular Housing Movement in São Paulo. Some 1,500 families occupied an empty plot and refused to move. Eventually the city council installed water and septic tanks for sewage disposal. Negotiations to transfer land titles to the squatters are progressing.*

with gusto a stirring apocalyptic anthem which had begun:

> When I saw the earth burning,
> What a fire of St John . . .

and which seemed much exercised with thoughts of divine retribution upon the rich and the wicked. As the police came into view they swiftly changed to a hymn of more luminous piety and from the front of the group of supporters stepped a lawyer from ANSUR who went to negotiate with the police chief. The singers were now well into the eighth-century hymn:

> Come Holy Spirit, fill the hearts of
> your faithful . . .

though mysteriously halfway through their rendition unfamiliar words began to appear, exhorting the Holy Spirit to 'inspire our struggle and enlighten the minds of our brothers in the police force'.

Before the negotiations were over the shed was complete. It was a magnificent edifice in the circumstances, thirty metres long and five metres wide. Some twenty families gave every appearance of being well-established, with children apparently sleeping peacefully beneath the soft hiss of the gas lamps and the smell of a hearty stew wafting from the stove. The policemen were invited in for coffee and to join in the ecumenical service which was about to begin, for which a Roman Catholic priest had mysteriously appeared with all the accoutrements of the altar. The police just looked around and had some coffee and then left.

'We picked a Friday night because there are no legal or public authorities working over the weekend. It gives us time to get established', said Miguel Borges Leal, one of the co-ordinators of the Housing Movement of the South East Zone which had organized the occupation of a patch of land owned by São Paulo state. 'The shed and its occupiers are a bridgehead for 1,000 families who want to come and live here. At present they live with inadequate space in *favelas* or they live in *corticos* they can no longer afford or they are already under order of eviction.'

Miguel's hope was that an organized group, backed by the local Catholic church and by lawyers from ANSUR, would do better than the spontaneous squat at Jardim da Saúde which had ended in failure. Within a few days the Vila Mariana community had established a committee which had opened negotiations with federal, state and city authorities over the land. 'That makes us feel safe here, at least for a while,' said Miguel.

Perhaps eventually they would succeed there, as Paulina and her friends had done at Casa Verde. Or perhaps, already, nobody lives on the stretch of scrubby land at Vila Marina any more. It would be strange to record the fact. Even now, perhaps, the site is empty.

Strengthening the Poor

Organizing for a better future

What makes people poor? This journey through three continents has made one thing abundantly clear. The desperate poverty in many parts of the world is not just the product of a collection of unhappy accidents caused by natural calamities. The fact that millions of people are not able to grow the food they need to feed themselves and their children is a crucial part of the problem.

Why cannot people grow enough to eat? Some are physically denied access to the soil, like those I met in the Philippines who had been evicted from the land on which their forebears had farmed for generations. Some have never been given an adequate amount of land because of population pressures; the first signs of this predicament were becoming evident among some of the families I met in Brazil but it is already a much more severe problem in other parts of the world, in countries like Bangladesh. Some, like the farmers of highland Eritrea, have established their right to land but, for other reasons, were unable to make that land produce enough to sustain a decent life.

This 'land trap' is to some extent the product of history. Over the past four hundred years the 'civilized' nations of Europe, and later North America, opened up the 'primitive' nations of the 'under-developed' world which we saw as a rich source of materials and, potentially, a huge market in which to sell our own goods. The process of colonization brought with it a scheme of thinking which is with us today in the very term 'Third World'. The First World was the West; the Second World was the Communist bloc; and the Third World, in which two-thirds of the world's population happens to live, was all the rest: it was as if they had come last in a race, which in some senses, of course, they have.

Colonialism set up an economic relationship in which the rich West had the whip-hand – sometimes all too literally – and which established the basic dynamic between the First and Third Worlds which still persists today. It also brought with it the racism which branded the indigenous peoples of the Third World as 'children before the law', savages incapable of deciding their own future. It took their land from them and created legal mechanisms which have left tribal people in both Brazil and in the Philippines outlaws in their own land.

Colonialism also altered the way land was used. All over Africa traditional systems for allocating land and ensuring that herds of animals did not become bigger than the pasture could sustain have been eroded, both by colonial administrators and then by the national organizations set up by newly independent governments. In much of Latin America and in southern and western Africa, huge plantations were created which forced peasant families out of systems of subsistence farming which had sustained their ancestors for generations. It robbed them of a way of life which allowed them to control their own daily existence and, in its place, established forms of slavery which, the accounts of the cocoa workers of Bahia revealed, have their echoes still in plantation life today.

In many countries the colonizers decided that

the cheapest and most effective way to control the native population was to strengthen the powers of the local ruling élites. This led, especially in parts of Asia, to the growth of a class of landowners who, over the years, have been able to extract rents at crippling levels from small farmers, often forcing them to surrender tenancies and work as landless labourers. The other contributing factor in the spread of landlessness has been the rapid growth in the population. Local custom in countries like Bangladesh dictates that when a man dies his property is divided among his children. So with every generation the plot of each individual becomes smaller. On such meagre plots the poor sustain themselves by only the barest of margins. When some quite minor emergency strikes, such as illness among the breadwinners, the poor often have to mortgage their land and eventually sell it just to stay alive.

But if the trap was built by history there can be no doubt that it is today made worse by the power and selfishness of wealthy Third World landowners and the thoughtlessness of those of us in the First World who, whether we realize it or not, benefit from the exploitation of millions of landless workers and sweat-shop labourers.

The responsibility of the rich in Third World countries is clear enough. In countries like Brazil and the Philippines the ordeals of the people I met at Utumuju and Imok, under threat of eviction from their land and homes, showed how every year the ownership of the land becomes more concentrated in the hands of an affluent local élite. The people I encountered in the slums of Manila, of São Paulo and of Rio de Janeiro showed how all this is forcing ordinary people to leave the countryside in large numbers for the squalor of urban shanty-towns. When political pressures become too intense and the demand for land reform becomes overwhelming, some concessions are made by the Third World rich

but then swiftly undermined, either by clever use of legal loopholes, as at the Hacienda Luisita, or by the use of private armies or thugs, a circumstance all too common in the Third World.

But we in the industrialized nations of the First world are complicit in all this too. As we have seen, the chocolate we eat has its price, subsidized by Maria and the other cocoa-pickers of Bahia, who cannot afford fresh vegetables for their children; their wages are squeezed as their bosses are forced into accepting low prices by a world market dominated by huge cocoa multinationals. Our high street banks force Third World countries to repay debts at crippling rates of interest; as a result Joã André and many other farmers were driven into the slums of São Paulo when their land was taken over for the production of export crops, like soya beans for animal fodder, to earn the foreign exchange needed to meet interest repayments. Our governments, through the mechanisms of the European Community, sell off our artificially-created food mountains at subsidized prices, lowering prices on world markets and thus ensuring that Third World farmers get less for their crops.

What, in the face of all this, can a charity like Christian Aid do to make some small impact on the mammoth task of improving the lot of the landless and the other poor?

'When you look at poverty you see that there is always something else there, besides material deprivation,' says Michael Taylor, the Director of Christian Aid. 'Being poor means having

OVERLEAF: *The fishermen of Lake Marawi in the Philippines are fighting the opening of a hydro-electric project which will cause the water level to drop. Farmers fear it will ruin their farms. Local people have formed an organization to lobby the government in Manila to axe the scheme.*

very little control over your own existence.' The decisions which govern the lives of the poor are made by other people. The moneylender, the employer, the multinational company, the government, foreign governments, the international finance bodies – all often have more say than do the poor themselves.

It was the same in Palestine in the first century A.D. 'In a World where the poor were unimportant Jesus repeatedly gave the impression that they are all central to God's concern. He touched and healed them, befriended and forgave them. He took people who were excluded from society and included them in his circle. He inspired in them a new sense of their worth. These people were not part of the problem, Jesus was saying, they are potentially the solvers of the problem. They need to be drawn in instead of excluded.'

One of the deep insights which the Christian tradition offers is that to have control of your own life, to participate in decisions about your future, is part of the fullness of humanity. 'Our moral duty towards the poor of the earth is to allow the poor to create and pursue their own values.'

According to Michael Taylor, helping the poor to achieve this new strength and self-confidence is a two-stage process. The first is to promote within them a greater understanding of their own poverty and its roots. 'When people develop a critique of their situation they develop an awareness of how to change it. But this is not knowledge which can be "delivered" to people; they have to work it out for themselves as part of a process of growth and self-discovery. It has to be from the bottom up, not from the top down.' The success of this technique was clear at Rora Habab in Eritrea where, despite the additional burden of a decade of drought, the women and men of the Christian Aid-supported project had found a new sense of self-confidence and self-worth which was infectious throughout the whole community.

The second step is to encourage people to come together to work for improvements in their lives. 'So they find ways to organize themselves, so that they lose the powerlessness of the individual and find their strength in one another.' This approach also bears fruit, as was evident from the new corporate sense of identity which had emerged among the Pataxó Hãhãhãi Indians in Brazil. It was also successful in the exchanges of information facilitated by the Cordillera Resource Centre in the mountain provinces of the Philippines where tribes now co-ordinate their activities in their attempts to hang on to their ancestral lands.

In many situations people's attempts to improve their lives in this way meets resistance from those powerful groups who are threatened by the new challenge. I encountered evidence of this in both the Philippines and Brazil where hundreds of church workers, human rights activists and trades union leaders have been killed in recent years by gunmen employed by landowners and land-grabbers. There was the sugar worker Alex, sleeping in a different bed every night in Tarlac to avoid assassins. There was Maria Lucia who slept with a gun beneath the blankets in her makeshift hut in a squat in São Paulo. There was the mother in Utumuju village still shivering with fear as she told how pistoleros had shot into the ground by her children's feet. It was sobering to think that such people could, any day, become such victims themselves.

'People want charities to be non-confrontational – indisputably kind and generous', says Michael Taylor. 'But if you want to tackle the root cause of poverty you have to do more. In the end land issues are issues of power and strength. If you're going to love your neighbour in a serious, non-sentimental way you have to face confrontation. It was something which Jesus did.'

Religious faith is something which invigorates the debate on land all over the Third World. Muslims in Eritrea and in the Philippines were reading and listening to the Koran with new eyes and ears as they debated the rights and wrongs of existing patterns of landholding. Christians in Brazil – like poor people throughout Africa, Asia and Latin America – were making new attempts to relate the Bible to their daily lives. As a result new forms of theology are arising which take more literally the meaning of the word – ways of speaking (*logia*) about God (*theo*).

Christians in Latin America have become even more specific; reflecting the growing importance of the issue of landlessness a number of thinkers there are currently at work on developing a 'Theology of Land'. Their approach is rooted in that of the continent's liberation theologians

In Adi Caieh in the highlands of Eritrea, Christian Aid funds a tree nursery. The seedlings this woman is planting will be part of a reafforestation project initiated, not by outsiders, but by local people.

whose 'Theology of Liberation' takes as its focal point the release of the Jews from their slavery in Egypt. Many Third World people see that event as a model for God's intention for the liberation of all the oppressed people's in the modern world.

This is of particular importance for an agency like Christian Aid whose work in helping the poor to strengthen themselves is rooted in a specifically Christian vision. The Peruvian priest and thinker Gustavo Gutiérrez calls this approach 'doing theology from the underside of history'. Jesus brought the Good News to the poor yet, in the past, too much thinking about the Gospel has been done by religious élites which formulated doctrines and then passed them down to the ordinary people. What is needed is the opposite – for religion to grow out of the experience of daily life – from the bottom up and not the top down. Theology, Gutiérrez says, 'rises only at sundown'. Out of the action of the day and the reading and reflection of the evening will come the plan for tomorrow's action. Only then will the Gospel become *of* the poor as well as *for* the poor.

It is hardly surprising, then, that when people without land begin to read the Bible for themselves one thing strikes them particularly – that the issue of land lies at the heart of much of the Old Testament. From the first, they point out, land was inextricably bound up with human identity – the very name of the first man comes from the Hebrew word for the soil, *'adamah*. It was at the core of the promise made by God to Abraham – that he and his descendants would have land. Jacob and his sons lost the land given by God when they abandoned it during a time of famine and sought refuge in Egypt, when eventually they were enslaved. This covenant was sealed by the Exodus when the People of God escaped a life of bondage in Egypt and were delivered into the Promised Land.

Live long in the land that the Lord swore to your ancestors to give them and to their descendants, a land flowing with milk and honey. For the land that you are about to enter is not like the land of Egypt, from which you have come, where you sow your seed and irrigate by foot like a vegetable garden. But the land that you are crossing over to occupy is a land of hills and valleys, watered by rain from the sky, a land that the Lord your God looks after. The eyes of the Lord your God are always on it, from the beginning of the year to the end of the year. *Deuteronomy 11:9–12*

Land continues as a central theme. When the Israelites begin to turn away from God much of the drift is expressed in terms of land – they find themselves a king, who changes the basis of land-holding in order to support his court, administration and armies. When the prophets arrive to criticize these developments much of their condemnation focuses on the abuse of land and the injustice of large land-holdings. And when the Israelites see themselves punished for these iniquities the punishment takes the form of the removal of land – Israel is conquered and its aristocracy taken off to exile in Babylon.

The importance attached to the land is clear from the fine and demanding detail of the rules and regulations drawn up to govern it in the early years of the Israelites' occupation of the Promised Land. A raft of specific injunctions about the land is recorded in the books of Leviticus and Deuteronomy. Biblical scholars disagree about whether they were all enforced in practice or whether they just constituted a counsel of perfection. Either way they are important because of the underlying philosophy they reveal.

The land belonged to God, and the community held it in trust on his behalf. The use of the land was allocated to individual families, not in accordance with their relative power or strength but by casting lots. They could not sell this land in perpetuity. They could sell the use of it, for a

number of harvests, but the original owner had the right to repurchase the land whenever he wanted. Moreover, in the Jubilee Year it had to be returned to the family to which it had originally been allocated. The Jubilee came every forty-nine years – a Sabbath's Sabbath. In that year all those poor men and women who had sold themselves into service were to be freed. These books of the Bible record many other general regulations. On ecological grounds the land had to be allowed to rest every seventh year when no cultivation was permitted and the poor could garner what grew. The migrant poor also had access to land through the right to a small share of all crops by gleaning at harvest-time.

Land here is much more than mere territory. It is more even than the wherewithal to grow food

This child worker looks after the mules which carry the cocoa beans down from the plantation slopes in Brazil. Such plantations often violate the working conditions laid down by law. The emergence of an effective regional union for cocoa workers, supported by one of Christian Aid's partners in Brazil, should help him assert his rights.

to sustain life. It is a mechanism through which justice is achieved. In the words of a theologian from the Amazon region, Narciso Farias: 'Land is not just the medium from which spring the crops which provide the food needed for the sustenance of life. Land is sacred. It is the space in which a person relates to God.' ·

All the detail of the Code of Leviticus adds up to an important vision. In a primitive agricultural community land was the basis of all economic relationships. Land was capital; land was your job. It was also the basis of social relationships. Land was status; it was a kind of membership card. To deprive someone of their land was to deprive them of both the means to live and the membership of a society which was the community of the People of God. 'To possess land was the same as living, to lose land was the equivalent of dying,' in the words of a lay theologian, Anna Maria Rizzante Gallazzi, from Macapá in the far north of Brazil.

The complex web of laws placed a stop on the accumulation of property in a few hands. And they ensured that the poor could never become trapped in a permanent cycle of deprivation which would rob them of part of their humanity.

'In the Exodus story, Egypt stands for a system where the benefits of land are monopolized by a feudal aristocracy for the benefit of a small elite; the Promised Land stands for a system where the benefits are for everyone,' says Father Lázaro Bruning, a parish priest from Cascavel in the west of Brazil who acts as chaplain to

Sugar workers in the Philippines have had their constitutional right to land reform neutered by manipulative landowners. Sentra, a citizens' advice group funded by Christian Aid, is helping them fight their case in the Philippine courts.

A Brazilian man dances with his child in a disco organized by the people of a slum community in Rio de Janeiro. They were raising money to stop a new highway cutting through their land, on which they had just successfully fought for water, electricity and sewage to be installed.

PREVIOUS PAGE: *Land reform alone is not enough to pull the poor farmer out of destitution. In Eritrea a scheme supported by Christian Aid at Rora Habab aims to provide an integrated programme of health, education, reafforestation, anti-erosion terracing and dam-building to give the peasants the back-up they need to make land reform work.*

a number of the local communities occupying land. 'Egypt stands for slavery, the Promised Land for freedom. Egypt means a life in which you were always told by someone else what to do; the Promised Land means a life where you could participate as an equal in the running of society.'

There are some places in which it is still possible today to operate the exact same systems which were first devised by the People of God when they arrived in the Promised Land. The villagers I met at Meshal in the highlands of Eritrea had preserved a system which has apparently been in operation since Christianity arrived there in the 4th century and, protected by the remoteness of the mountains, has remained untouched ever since. Land tenure still retains elements of that Levitical code: land is the property of the community and is distributed to individuals who have the right to use it but do not own it; there is a mechanism of redistribution to maintain a sense of fairness in society and prevent the accumulation of land in the hands of a wealthy few; the land is even distributed by lot.

The recent extension of that system, which gave land to women and to residents who were not born there, illustrated the close relationship between owning land and being a full member of society. As one of the former landless, Gidav Gebre Selassie, told me: 'Before I think people had a regard for me but I was always an outsider. Now at the age of sixty-five I am at last an equal. It is only when you have your own land that you are a proper man.'

But it would be unrealistic to suppose that such literal applications of biblical practices would be appropriate now for most of the world's poor. 'No-one is suggesting that all of this must actually be implemented in this concrete way today in the Third World,' says Ana Flora Anderson, who works with a group of theologians in São Paulo, who have begun the task of uncovering a Theology of Land. 'We don't have the same economic system as in those days. But the texts are an appeal to our time. We have to understand them as a prophetic appeal. We have to uncover the principles which underlie them.'

Those principles require a system of land-holding which promotes social justice and nurtures the dignity of each individual. They require social systems which prevent people from being permanently deprived of the means to earn a living. They require structures to be built into the economy which establish self-righting mechanisms to prevent the poor from becoming destitute and to prevent the rich from exploiting the predicament of the poor. But, say those working on a Theology of the Land, the biblical

situations are realistic as well as idealistic. 'The Promised Land was not *given* to the Israelites', notes Natalia Soares – who works in the north-east region of Brazil, where the landowners and their gunmen are perhaps more violent and ruthless than anywhere else in the world. 'They had to fight for it. The Promised Land was not simply occupied, it was conquered,' she says, pointing out that the city states of the Canaanites defeated by the Israelites were symbols of feudal exploitation just as Egypt was. The poor today must also expect to have to struggle for reform, organizing themselves into groups strong enough to insist on what is due to them.

Most liberation theologians would see such a conclusion as inevitable. Given the nature of the lives of the poor any theology they develop themselves will have political, social and economic components which may demand radical change. Such change is bound to be resisted by the powerful. The poor will only achieve it if they come together to find the new strength which will force the powerful to listen. Interestingly enough the recent history of land reform points to a similar conclusion.

There is nothing new about the idea of land reform. Nor is there anything new about wide-scale redistribution of land rights in the twentieth century. There have been major changes in the way land is held in a number of countries, precipitated usually by revolutions, wars or independence from colonial rule. Significant transformatons have occurred in Japan, South Korea and Taiwan as well as in the former Soviet Union, China, and many African countries. But the changes have often done very little to improve the life of the mass of poor people in those countries.

At one extreme, revolutions swept away the old

landed order in the Soviet Union, China, North Korea, Vietnam, Mexico, Cuba and Ethiopia. But all too often the result was not to give ordinary people control of the land they farmed. Most twentieth century socialist governments saw peasants as inefficient and unreliable in their political allegiance. So instead they set up large-scale collective farms with modern technology, where peasants resented the changes. They have proved a dismal failure. To make matters worse these governments taxed agriculture heavily to fund industrialization or, in the case of corrupt regimes, to provide privileges for the elite.

Many attempts to introduce more gradualist programmes of reform have also failed. In the 1960s the Kennedy administration in the United States inaugurated an Alliance for Progress designed to bring land reform to Latin America. The aim of the US government was to offer enough reform to prevent the growth of popular dissatisfaction which might lead to communist revolutions in its 'backyard'. It failed for a number of reasons. It was undermined by local elites who appeared to comply (to appease their powerful friends in Washington) but who behind the scenes resisted any change which would lessen their wealth or power. Much of the land earmarked for reform in countries like Bolivia was actually given to the cronies of the government for livestock raising and industrial forestry. In other countries, where land was given to the poor, the scheme foundered because

Two semi-nomadic goat-herds in Eritrea. Christian Aid is funding a project there to restock the herds of those worst hit by drought. Animal health care programmes try to encourage the nomads to have fewer goats – but of better quality. The aim is to prevent overgrazing and environmental damage.

subsequent government policies were biased against the peasant. Tax incentives and subsidized credit were designed to favour big agribusiness rather than to raise productivity in smallholder agriculture. And general agricultural policy was – and still is – more often aimed at trying to keep prices down to provide cheap food for the towns rather than to pay fair prices to farmers.

Were these the only cases of land reform, the outlook for the world's landless would be bleak, but there are instances of reform which did make the poor noticeably better off. In China, where a sixth of the world's population have experienced two enormous upheavals in landholding systems in the last fifty years, a country which was once a byword for famine has now virtually eliminated it. The first change, under the revolution of Chairman Mao, turned the land over from landlords to collectives of farmers. By the 1980s the state realized that the collectives were inefficient, and handed most of the land over to individual families; production rose forty per cent as a result.

Improvements in living standards occurred after more gradual reforms in Taiwan and South Korea. The programme in Taiwan was conducted along the lines of the agrarian reform conducted in Japan under the American occupation after the end of the Second World War. It, like the one in South Korea, created a more equitable distribution of assets in the countryside. This provided new incentives for agriculture and liberated the money which farmers had previously paid in rent to be invested in increased production. Both countries were then able to build outward-orientated industrial economic strategies on the new growth in the countryside, turning Taiwan and South Korea into two of the most dynamic of the world's developing nations.

Another notable land reform success was in Kerala State in India, where an ineffective state government in a federated system enabled well-organized peasant groups to influence events. This was a key factor, as indeed it had been in South Korea and Taiwan. In each case the reform was not simply decreed by some well meaning regime. Rather, landed élites there did not have control over the state, and reform was conceded by the authorities under pressure from the growing strength of peasant organizations, much as it had been in China. It was through being well organized and by using this economic and political muscle that they have achieved, and maintained, real gains under the law. The message is that where small farmers are strong enough to protect their own interests, land reforms can succeed.

For an agency like Christian Aid three key factors now point in a single direction. First, the Gospel requires that Christians in the First World afford their sisters and brothers in the Third World the dignity of involving them in the making of decisions. Secondly, those poor people, from their own experience and the theology which springs from it, ask for help to build the organizations which will allow them to demand their rights. Thirdly, experience of land reform shows that it only works when those who demand it are in a position of strength.

Putting all this into practice on the ground is a complex task. 'It means we have to look for projects to fund which work on many different levels at once,' says Paul Spray, the Head of Aid for Christian Aid. The agency has therefore established a number of guidelines. A project should alleviate suffering but it should do more – it should also in some way contribute towards actually ending suffering. It should help people gain greater understanding of why and how they are poor and oppressed. It should bring people together, building organizations among the most vulnerable groups – the very poorest, the women, and the oppressed ethnic minorities. It should show respect for the environment. It should in some way promote distributive justice rather than creating a group which becomes much better off than its peers.

'On the question of land there are two issues which intertwine inseparably. One is concerned with helping poor people gain control of the land. The other is concerned with making it produce more, in a way which is ecologically sound and sustainable. So to tackle the problem two approaches are needed – one which helps peasants gain control, by strengthening their organizations, and one which helps them raise productivity.

'Neither approach would be effective on its own as the two issues interrelate. If we concentrated simply on helping to improve farming yields the people who would benefit most would be the landowners, not the poor. On the other hand, even genuine land reforms are rapidly eroded if the peasants who gain the land don't gain the wherewithal and technology to make the land produce enough. All over the world Christian Aid is supporting projects which aim to help poor farmers increase their incomes: in the Amazon we help peasants to develop better farming methods and then spread them to others; in Malawi we work with a group which is introducing new methods of sustainable agriculture to women's groups; in Bangladesh we support an institute which is investigating improved crops, animals and markets for a group of people who have recently won land after a decade's struggle.'

Ideally Christian Aid chooses projects which combine the dual aims – of strengthening organization and of improving productivity – in a single enterprise. Sentra in the Philippines provides a legal advice service to peasants trying to use the courts to challenge the attempts of landowners to dispossess them. But, having discovered that being right under the law is often not sufficient, it is now beginning to place equal emphasis on the need to organize peasant groups so that their legal challenges are backed up with pressure on the ground. Such pressure would be impossible without the economic strength which derives from the improved productivity produced by having access to technical advice, agricultural loans, co-operative buying power and better marketing systems.

In Bangladesh, where there is just not enough land to go around, the answer to the people's problems cannot consist solely in land reform. There Christian Aid's partners combine pressure for fairer land distribution with efforts to raise the productivity of the land, and to promote other, non-farming, ways the poor can earn a living.

In Brazil the landless movement Sem Terra has a similar dual function. It provides agricultural advice to peasant farmers who have just acquired land or who are in danger of losing it to the banks with which they have built up debts. But it also organizes groups of the landless in occupations of unused land, and offers legal services to help peasants negotiate with local authorities for the land to be expropriated under existing land reform laws.

In the final analysis, however, the problems of land cannot be solved in the Third World alone. 'This is why we have sponsored research on subjects such as how Third World farmers are affected by the Common Agricultural Policy and publicized the way that the Gatt trade talks neglect the best interests of the poor', says Michael Taylor. 'People in the industrialized nations have to understand that we are part of the problem. The effects of unfair trade or of Third World debt have to be explained to people here, because they are not immediately obvious. Because without changes at these macro-levels the micro change we are working for with small projects on the ground will be meaningless.'

The greatest engine of injustice is an imbalance

of strength. 'Ultimately everything we do is aimed at lessening that disparity. We can appeal to the rich to give the poor the access to the land they need. But in the end we shall not be surprised if they refuse to give up part of their wealth and power. That is why we must do our part to strengthen the organizations of the poor. So that the powerful will one day be obliged to hear their demand for justice.'

That demand echoes from the rocky plateaux of Eritrea. It rings from the mountains of the Indian people in the Philippines. It resounds from the remote hillside of the Atlantic rainforest in Brazil where 81-year-old Estacio Alejandré Cruz had concluded: 'Justice is not a matter of pieces of paper . . . . God gave the land for everyone. How can one person own the land? The land is here forever, but our lives are short.

To secure the continuance of their tribe the Pataxó Hãhãhãi must preserve their ancient ways. But they must also develop new techniques to ensure the Brazilian government honours its commitment to protect their rights. Christian Aid funds Cimi, an organization which builds alliances between them and other Indian groups.

It is the land which owns the individual, not the other way around.'

But, after a journey across three continents over a period of almost a year, the demand of the poor for justice reverberated most powerfully for me in the words of the woman I could not name. Maria, I had called her, because she was too frightened to give her real name, supposing that if her identity was known she would lose her job as a cocoa harvester on the plantation of Fazenda Agua Branca outside the town of Wenceslau Guimarães in the middle of Bahia, Brazil.

We had met deep in the forest of cocoa trees. She had thought I was a buyer from one of the multi-national cocoa-processing firms which set the terms under which she laboured.

'Raise the minimum wage', she had said. 'We work hard here, but we do not get enough to live off. We get some wage rises but the price rises are always more and faster I have nine small children to feed. They are not getting enough to eat. My husband is ill and cannot work. I cannot afford the medicine for him. We work hard, but we do not get enough to live.'

Maria was not asking for charity. She was not asking for aid. She was asking for a fair wage for her back-breaking day's work. She was asking for justice.

I had thought our conversation was over, for it seemed there was nothing left to say. The canopy of leaves above me suddenly felt oppressive and

I walked on through the forest of cocoa trees until I came upon a clearing bathed in a shaft of sunlight. The air felt fresher there and the waxy leaves of the cocoa trees shone in the bright sunlight as if they had been polished.

There was a cough behind me. It was Maria. She stood for a moment in the pool of light. Her tattered shirt, which had looked dirty and dingy in the gloom of the undergrowth, now looked brilliantly colourful, and the yellow cocoa pods in the large basket slung from her shoulder glinted like gold in the sunshine. She smiled, for the first time, and produced from behind her a small bundle, wrapped in an old cloth.

'You have come far into the plantation with no food,' she said, 'It is lunchtime.' Swinging the basket down to the ground she squatted on a fallen tree and untied the corners of the cloth. Inside was a ball of sticky yellow-white porridge. 'It is *farofa*, cassava flour mixed with palm oil', she said, and began to chat to cover my silence. 'There is no beans or meat, I am afraid. Cold beans are bad for the digestion; they bring stomach ache. And meat, I am sorry, but we hardly talk about meat these days. But the *farofa* is good. Come eat. It is good to share.'

I looked at the small mound of food. Embarrassed, I began to mutter that I was not hungry.

'Nonsense', she replied. 'It is a long way back to the town. I have food; you have none. It is my duty to share with you.' She pulled a lump from the yellowy ball and held it out to me.

Acknowledgements

On the Philippines journey thanks to Margaret O'Grady and Catherine Matheson at Christian Aid; to Linda Mclintock, Sheila Coronel, Steve Alston and Caroline Spires. In the Philippines thanks to Laarni Valerio, Joel Rodriguez, Marvic Leonen, Sr Christine Tan, Meling Ogania, Mike Macarambon, Hajji Omar Faisal, and Gerry Fiagoy.

On the Eritrea journey thanks to Sarah Hughes at Christian Aid; to Berhane Ghebrehiwot at ERA in London and Goytom Woldemariam at ERA in Colognel to Trish Silkin and Stephen King. In Khartoum thanks to Jonas Debessay; to Gayle Smith; and to all the staff of the Acropole Hotel. In Eritrea thanks to Ghirmai Asmerom, Goytem Keshi-Mussie, Tsehaye Gaim, Haile Menkerios, Osman Idris and Asha Mohamed Said, and Abba Yissak Gebreyesus. Special thanks to Gebremariam Goytom and Letenk'iel Berake who welcomed us into their home for a week and to CAFOD who lent us a vehicle for five weeks.

On the Brazil journey thanks to Wendy Tyndale, Domingos Armani, and Larry Boyd of Christian Aid, and to Clare Dixon and Francis McDonagh. In Brazil thanks to Mike Bailey, Alonso Roberts, Jeff Williams, William van Volsen, José Miguel da Silva, Jan Rocha, Fr Lazaro Bruning, Ana Flora Anderson, Sister Michael Mary Nolan, Helené Lackenbauer, Elza Maria Gheller, José Geraldo Rocha, Carlos Belle, Mera Costa and Luis Carlos.

Thanks to Giles Semper at Harper Collins *Publishers* and to Martina Crowley, Kate Phillips, Brenda Knight, Angela Burton, Paul Spray and Michael Taylor at Christian Aid for general assistance. Thanks to Nigel Horne, editor of the *Daily Telegraph Magazine* and Trevor Grove, editor of the *Sunday Telegraph*, who funded part of the travel. Thanks to Seamus Heaney for 'Digging' from *Death of a Naturalist* (Faber & Faber).

Thanks to Heather Vallely for a careful reading of the manuscript, and a lot more.